COMPUTER
EPISTEMOLOGY

WORLD SCIENTIFIC SERIES IN COMPUTER SCIENCE

For a complete list of published titles in the series, please write in to the publisher.

World Scientific Series in Computer Science – Vol. 25

COMPUTER EPISTEMOLOGY

A Treatise on the Feasibility of the Unfeasible or Old Ideas Brewed New

Tibor Vámos

Computer and Automation Institute
Hungarian Academy of Sciences
Budapest, Hungary

World Scientific

Singapore • New Jersey • London • Hong Kong

Published by

World Scientific Publishing Co. Pte. Ltd.
P O Box 128, Farrer Road, Singapore 9128
USA office: 687 Hartwell Street, Teaneck, NJ 07666
UK office: 73 Lynton Mead, Totteridge, London N20 8DH

Library of Congress Cataloging-in-Publication Data

Vámos, Tibor.
    Computer epistemology : a treatise on the feasibility of the unfeasible or old
ideas brewed new / Tibor Vámos.
        p.   cm.   -- (Series in computer science ; vol. 25)
    Includes bibliographical references and index.
    ISBN 9810203500.
    1. Computer science.   2. Artificial intelligence.   I. Title.
II. Series.
QA76.V325   1990
004--dc20   90-47680
                                                                     CIP

Printed in Singapore by JBW Printers & Binders Pte. Ltd.

Acknowledgement of contributions

This work was supported by:

    The National Science Foundation of Hungary (OTKA)

    International Synergy Institute, Los Angeles, CA

Editorial work of English styling by:

    Allyn B. Brodsky, managing editor

Figures by:

    Hilda Kozári, artist

except:		
Preface left	–	A sketch of *Jacob Spon*, French archeologist, after a Roman relief (Miscellanea Eruditae Antiquitatis, 1679)
2.7	–	*A. Schmid*: Christliche Symbole aus alter und neuer Zeit, Herder Verlag, 1909
3.3, 5.10	–	K. Kovács, applying the figures of *Jean Effel* and the Scientific American respectively
4.2, 4.3a	–	*F. Schuyl*, in Œuvres de Descartes, Traité de l'homme, ed. M. Clerselier, Paris, 1664
4.4b	–	*Jonathan Swift*: Gulliver's Travels, printed for Benj. Motte, London, 1726 (repr. Oxford: Basil Blackwell, 1959)
4.7, 5.8, 5.13	–	The Computer Is Also Human, International Competition for Cartoons, J. von Neumann Society for Computing

Sciences, Budapest, 1988: T. Kaján, A. Mészáros and Neshaev respectively

5.12   – *E. H. Shepard*, in A. A. Milne: Winnie-the-Pooh, Menthuen, London, 1926

Conclusion   – Miniature from Hortus Deliciarium of Herrad, abbess of Landsberg, 1175 (repr. Lexikon christlicher Kunst, Herder Verlag, Freiburg im Breisgau 1980)

Typesetting by:
    Gy. Hetényi and Gy. Visontay
    Computer and Automation Institute,
    Hungarian Academy of Sciences
    Budapest

Contents

Contents

Contents

Preface

Accipe haec aetas

This book is neither a textbook nor a monograph, but an essay. The style is defined by the subject and the objective. The subject matter lies in an area between computer science and philosophy, while the objective is to offer something between a general overview and practical advice. An essay is the form best suited for a work of this intermediate nature.

The thoughts presented here are the results of extensive practical experience: a decade in computer process control using large scale systems, another decade in machine pattern recognition for vision systems, and nearly a decade dealing with artificial intelligence and expert systems. These real-life projects have taught me a critical appreciation of and respect for both abstract theory and the practical methodology which grows out of—and, in turn, shapes—those theories. As I dealt with the basic problems of large scale systems modelling and control, my professional career, although seemingly diverse to an observer, led to this balanced view of the pros and cons of theory and practice.

From that perspective, this essay can be read as a philosophical reflection on large scale systems' practice, but this mirror also works in the opposite direction as well, as do most of our meditations. That is a natural aspect of any approach to the Unreachable. Studying the philosophical background, nowadays mostly forgotten in the literature of Artificial Intelligence, I could find practically all the most recent technical ideas, presented more or less clearly, as far back as Greek Antiquity. As will be discussed in further detail, the flourishing of Greek Philosophy about the 3rd Century B.C., Medieval Science, especially the British schools of the 12-14th century, and the Age of Reason, the 17-18th century, have all contributed tremendously to those ideas about truth and falsity on which we now base our computer algorithms. This discovery was another lesson in modesty, and a further stimulus to reach back as far as possible in the history of human thinking. Often the *process* of progress, the stories of unanswered questions, are as instructive as the phylogenetic processes of evolution. Nevertheless, as an essay this book is not intended as a survey of philosophy. It uses only those citations which were found to fit the essence of what I wanted to say. That essence is really the balanced viewpoint I described above.

Our century has been filled with great, messianic promises and equally profound disappointments. This has happened not only in politics, in economics and technology, but can also be seen in the rapid changes and controversial directions of various arts. Ours is not the only century to claim first place in many aspects of life. As we have learned in systems science, nonlinear behavior leads to chaotic disorder, and can reach new equilibria only by going through excessive perturbations.

One major vehicle of this century's technological progress is computer science. At its heart lie those efforts which could be modestly characterized as automatized support for human work, but are more commonly known as *artificial intelligence*. All kinds of extreme views and perspectives on AI can be found in the literature, both in philosophy and computer science, but also in sociology, psychology and science fiction as well. This essay should be seen as a contribution to this on-going discussion, one that consists of both experience and insight, as described above.

For whom is it written? Textbooks are written for students or those who would like to become acquainted with another field of knowledge related to their own work. Monographs are usually intended for a close circle of those who have special expertise; popular books aim for a very broad audience interested in some exciting new topic. An essay is written first for the author, as a device for organization and clarification of his own *Weltanschauung.*[*] In the closest circle around this narcissistic center are those who have had similar thoughts and experiences, and the essay can be helpful to them in the further organization and clarification of these shared concerns. The next circle of the audience includes all those who have some professional interest in the topic as developers, users, or others concerned in some way. This determines the core content: a progressive, optimistic, appreciative, but critical view of the achievements and perspectives of our technology (modestly, I use the term *technology* here instead of *science*). If we would look for an attribute in the macrosphere, this is the traditional liberal-humanistic view. Winking at those circles the reader finds an explanation of the confused usage of pronominal forms: I, we, somebody, anybody, etc. *We* return to that in the conclusion.

The prior knowledge required is a fuzzy concept as well. No author can be sure about these requirements except those who only write textbooks for students in a familiar curriculum and who have continuous feedback from the students as well. Nevertheless, something like an M.A. in computer science is assumed, or equivalent experience. Literacy of a similar level, and the humanistic interests of a responsible intellectual are also presupposed. The Appendix is intended to bridge some gaps by suggesting slightly more technical insights concerning the

---

[*] "A comprehensive world view, especially from a specified standpoint" — The American Heritage Dictionary

concepts discussed, but never with the aim of providing complete instruction in the methodology.

It may be surprising that no math is used although the topic is deeply related to mathematics. I hope that the reason for this is clear from what has been said above.

This book was stimulated by several people. The organization of the chapters and content is due first to *Dimitris Chorafas*, who organizes an annual meeting on Artificial Intelligence in West Berlin: *Robert Trappl* in Vienna invited me to discussions where I had the opportunity to meet *Michael Arbib, Nils Nilsson, Margaret Boden*, among others, and observe their attitudes to the problems concerned. I was influenced by *Judea Pearl* of UCLA, with whom I had personal talks and much correspondence, by friendly personal contacts with *Donald Michie* of the Turing Institute, by the works of *Hilary Putnam, Hubert* and *Stuart Dreyfus, Morris Kline, Douglas Hofstadter* and many other mathematicians, philosophers, psychologists, and contemporary computer scientists writing about related problems. Sometimes I have been influenced even more by authors of the past, a long sequence of human thinking about the same fundamental questions, manifested for them in the mirror of their relations, the encounters of their ages. I learned a lot from my colleagues, especially from *F. Bródy*, a philosopher-mathematician, *László Mérő*, a cognitive psychologist-mathematician, *Lajos Rónyai*, a mathematician, and *Márta Fehér*, a philosopher of science. *Andra Akers* read this book in an earlier version and supported the English styling by the generosity of the International Synergy Institute, Los Angeles, CA. This work was completed by *Allyn B. Brodsky* in a record time and in an admirable empathic way. *Jennifer Gan* was my superior and careful editor. *Hilda Kozári* drew most of the illustrations emphasizing the contrast between an easy superficial style of treatise and an earnest subject. The desk top editorial work was helped by *György Visontay*. A major acknowledgement should be made to *Gyöngyi Hetényi* who took care of the whole book and of me.

Is there anything new in this book? I doubt it; my statements reflect eternal questions, and the experiences I have collected, whether of others or my own, are, I believe, similar to those of anybody who is working in this field. Nevertheless, equally true is the statement from Ecclesiastes (the Book of The Preacher): "All the rivers run into the sea, Yet the sea is not full; Unto the place whither the rivers go, Thither they go again." (1:7) "The thing that has been, it is *that* which shall be; and which is done, is that which shall be done; and *there is* no new *thing* under the sun." (1:9)

Accipe posteritas — posterity, please accept — was the dedication of the Latin poet; **accipe haec aetas** — contemporary, please accept — this is what I ask. Accept this work with an attitude of liberal goodwill and help me and all the circles of our audience to organize and clarify our views!

Introduction

Utensil or Golem* — Master or Zauberlehrling?**

 If somebody entrusts all his property to somebody else, he does it carefully, with much consideration, even if his trustee is his closest friend. After taking this action he is dependent on the trustworthiness, wisdom, prudence, even good luck of his partner.

This is just our historical situation at the moment. We are starting to trust our greatest wealth, our knowledge, to a new partner that never before existed, computers. We are about to let them manage this wealth more or less on our behalf. We have to comprehend the responsibilities entailed by this action, to consider every factor which can be considered and examine both risks and safety. That is the reason why our seemingly theoretical-philosophical theme is as practical as anything else we chose to think about. It is also the reason why an engineer like myself — whose career has paralleled a rapid, unexpected, but logical development in technology, as described in the preface — turns his attention to basic consequences, formerly a privilege of philosophers.

This moment — as every moment in history — refers to analogous ones. There are three earlier revolutions in our history which share some crucial similarity with this one. These are all revolutions in human

---

* Golem: In Jewish folklore an artificially created human being endowed with life by supernatural means.

** Zauberlehrling (Sorcerer's apprentice): *Goethe*'s symbolic poem on a youngster who learnt how to bring the spirits about but not how to control and put them aside.

communication, i.e. in ways by which knowledge has been propagated: the evolution of *language*, the development of *writing*, and the invention of *printing*.

Revolution is as relative a concept as others — we shall discuss it further in Sections 4.2 and 4.5. One main feature of human information revolutions is the fact and manner by which man *sets the media of information outside of the self*. The result is that biological means of organization, inheritance, and selection are superseded. Information organizes cooperation to a much greater extent than simple physical coexistence. It bridges generations, and, through the rise and fall of concepts, maxims, or paradigms, it accomplishes a form of natural selection without biological instruments. The revolutions of information media enumerated are selected by this criterion.

The *propagation of knowledge* is a thorny issue. It contains the profound experience that perception of knowledge starts with communication, i.e. with a reflection from other conscious beings of how he/she understood our ideas. The reflection, the mirror, is one of the oldest metaphors: We gain an impression of ourselves by looking at a mirror, initially, at the smooth surface of still water. This primal communication is intended to initiate some kind of cooperation, actions that should be the same as our thoughts.

Cooperation based on some early kinds of communication has a long history as well, starting with animal life. But why it fails, why — as we would now formulate the process — the partner's model as a basis for responses is different from our own, and how this process can be improved, these are the real human advancements.

In the beginning no formularization of thoughts was needed and no feedback control was used to check the validity of this formularization. The new requirement began a long, multifaceted development of theory, which has been an extremely practical device for all organized activities, especially those requiring cooperation by communication. On the other hand, this line of theoretical development has led to a perpetual departure from the practical by encouraging the building of transcendental world structures. This is the history of ideologies. The analogy to the four communication revolutions is obvious: facing the new needs of formularization, of thinking about the nature of our mind, about thought processes, and about the relationship of *reality* and *representation*. Representation is understood both as representation in our mind and representation in the means of communication; the difference between the two was also perceived very early in human history and was disputed then as well as nowadays.

This representation process led to the use of *symbols*, and so to the evolution of hierarchies of symbols which mark conceptual thinking. The metalevels of those intellectual phenomena will be discussed in detail later. Yet the process has also led to the possibility of high-level communication and to the unsolvable problems of such communication. The semi-independent life of the representation evoked reflectivity, the relativity of self and alien references.

The dissimilarities of these four revolutions, their sequential nature, and their consequences are equally relevant. One major feature is the radius of effective action. The spoken language originally was directed to encompass a small circle of people, with direct feedback of many types of metacommunication. Nevertheless, we know that this early *language* has shown the mentioned bifurcation between practical cooperation and escape into transcendental structures. Despite having a practical value in avoiding dangers and organizing cooperation for acquiring vital needs, language was believed to be magical. Names became taboos, as the name of God was to the ancient Jews, or were used as witchery to expel evil. The representation started to live its own eccentric life.

More important for our metaphors is the second revolution, *writing*. Writing excluded any further means of metacommunication. It broke the direct link between the emitter of the message and the receiver. The representation had to carry the entire intended content. Writing extended the human memory to an infinite capacity — both limited and unlimited by the capabilities of the language and human comprehension. This means that the written information has no physical limits but several intellectual ones on both sides: the emitter and the receiver.

These achievements and features brought forth the origins of science as we understand it in our European culture. Later in this book, referring to the philosophy of the classic Greeks, we shall see how they met practically the same problems as we do now — under very different conditions, of course.

The transcendental life of communication and its media continued. The holy books of each religion embodied the ruling ideology that all of them attributed to a divine origin, but all contained very practical rules of human cooperation as well.

The third revolution, *printing*, diverted the course of communication into wide distribution. The books of Antiquity were intended for distribution as well, across both space and time. But they were useful among a very small circle of erudite people, those who had the same culture, language, and references. The books of Aristotle were compiled mostly by students, reminding us of recent lecture notes that supplement live talks to a group. Printing opened the whole world to different ideas, just as the world itself was widening into the present Universe, allowing the circulation of thoughts to incorporate new masses. This ability to broadcast ideas, combined with the achievements of the New Science, the ability to influence the dynamics of physical processes and of societies, renewed the confrontation of knowledge and representation. It can be argued that the effects of printing were minor compared with the innovations of science, so that possibly we may dismiss this dispute as futile. In this introduction, however, we try to emphasize those aspects which lead us to the comprehension why we meet similar problems through the millennia, and why the answers are necessarily and simultaneously similar and different.

We have arrived at the fourth revolution of communication. *Computers and electronic communication* are different from all previous means due to their immense capacity for storage and transmission, their speed in achieving direct connections and feedback. This feedback may be most important from our point of view: a feedback which does not come directly from another human being but from a machine, or at least via a machine which performs substantial transformations on human messages.

Such feedback can become a disastrous hitback. This is also the case in relationships among people — the entire record of human history is a record of conflicts due to contradictions of models (beliefs, ideologies) with Reality. Nevertheless people were used to it, both the blessings of cooperation and the disasters of conflict were acknowledged as nature's behavior, God's reward or punishment. The novelty of this new agent of history and its daily actions has not yet been absorbed and is far from being understood in its totality.

At each turn of human thinking, a new perspective arose on the relationship between reality and representation, on the truth or falsity of facts. At each turning-point, these basic and seemingly final concepts were questioned, this ability to look at ourselves and the world from outside was and is our most human feature. Can we, in fact, distinguish a separation between 'ourselves' and the world? If yes, at least to some extent, then what are the borders and what remains inseparable? These were always basic problems of philosophy. Communication and representation (by words, figures, mime, touch, colors, etc.) are just at the edges of such simultaneous borders and connections. If they were perfect processes, they could help to mediate the cooperation of the human universe (mankind and its environment) in an optimal way. (This concept of optimality is also a much debatable one.) We see and shall speak about in this book more that any perfect relation is impossible, the conflicts are therefore unavoidable. Just the conflict is the major way of cooperative understanding. In this light can we speak about an optimal way, a lowest sacrifice.

We are sometimes struck by the dullness of an answering machine, even more by that of a computerized information system which can lead or mislead us toward a promising direction of knowledge, then suddenly fail to go on. We feel a rigidity in machine communication, although the human attendant can be just as dull. But she/he looks more transparent because there are other features to which both we and they have been socialized. A smile, a vague attempt to help further, a feeling of sympathy or even antipathy — having a living culprit can resolve the situation. The loss of these protections of human communication may seem negligible compared to the consequences of more intelligent machines. Yet it is a bit similar to the controversy that might develop when we meet inadequate humans or a sophisticated but insanely insensible bureaucracy.

The *intelligent machine* is just starting to gain a certain power in our lives. Its calculations, decision technique, and reasoning will have an increasing role in anything that happens to us. It calculates our financial status, creditability, or traffic speed, evaluates the functions of our body and thus influences decisions on health, medical operations, or other vital interventions. It controls dangerous equipments, machines such as airplanes, nuclear power stations, and other indispensable services. We can say that the most delicate applications are not completely autonomous. They are supervised by men, but this is increasingly misleading. Several kinds of processes are too fast to be taken over by satisfactory human control. The system itself and the operators themselves are too accustomed to the automatic regime to make this switch. Human life becomes increasingly machine dependent. The information flow is a self-generating process, the possibility of high speed and high capacity information processing has created systems which issue and require an information flow beyond the human capacities.

Related to this dramatic change is the *complexity* of computer-operated systems. This complexity is different from that which was once resolved by the human intellect. The solutions of traditional and computerized systems are diverging, due to the differing abilities of the human brain and the computer. We shall return to this subject later, because it is one of our main issues. Here we only would like to show why the relationships of human and computer thinking must be investigated, what new factors have been added to the old problem of mind and reality, facts and their representations.

One can argue that even in the most intelligent knowledge-based system there is nothing other than human reasoning and human experience, programmed by reliable experts for even more reliable machines. We shall discuss how fallible this statement is, how much of reality is lost by computer representation, and how fallible the computer's further steps are.

As developers of *knowledge-based* and *computer-controlled systems* we are not arguing against them. We could not do it even if we were sure of the harm they can do. Computer-controlled systems containing more and more knowledge, executing more and more sophisticated tasks, are progressing rapidly and they provide much help, as well as challenge, to mankind. Unavoidably we trust ever more of our activities and knowledge to computers, and they feed those back to us, processed and transformed, influencing even more our further activities and knowledge.

In the course of this processing of millions, billions, and even greater orders of magnitude more operations we can loose insight and control. Impressed by this mighty power, we can feel a deceptive feeling of certainty about the outcome, the soundness of machine operation, the objectivity of the procedure.

All these perspectives shed new light on the representation problem of philosophy. The ancient and recurring doubts of philosophy change now to practical questions of engineering applications: What is, in fact, what we use as input for computer-controlled systems of any kind and what happens with them during processing? What is the relation of the output to our desires, imagination, needs?

Epistemology is the ancient Greek name for the discipline that studies knowledge, derived, in fact from the Greek words for discourse about knowledge. Many attempts have been made to distinguish the human from animals—we shall return to the fallibility of those attempts later—but according to our view we must share the aphoristic opinion of *Theilhard de Chardin*: "The animal knows, of course, But it certainly does not know that it knows." According to this definition, the question of how our knowledge relates to reality, understanding this basic difference, was the very start of human thinking. Reflecting on the self and knowledge, on the self and reality, originated the typical mental detachment of humans, the ambiguous wobbling between doubts and beliefs. What we would like to summarize here is the status of this eternal human quest — eternal in human terms yet made new by a new agent, the computer. We restrict ourselves to those issues most closely related to this novelty and that is the reason why we shall return to the historical origins at several points, trying to provide a special, historical emphasis to update the issue in the light of the current context. That special emphasis is provided by the title: **computer epistemology**.

Knowledge-based computer systems — although the denotations, the definitions are clumsy, liable to subjective, transient tendencies — are classified as areas of Artificial Intelligence. The relationship between AI and philosophy started with the birth of AI. *J. Haugeland* [1985] quotes *Thomas Hobbes* (1588-1679) about the very idea of Artificial Intelligence: "By ratiocination, I mean computation." A seminal paper of *McCarthy* and *Hayes* in 1969 gives a still valid answer to their question: "Why does artificial intelligence need philosophy?"

"The right way to think about the general problems of metaphysics and epistemology is not to attempt to clear one's own mind of all knowledge and start with 'Cogito ergo sum' and build up from there. Instead, we propose to use all of our own knowledge to construct a computer program that knows. The correctness of our philosophical system will be tested by numerous comparisons between the beliefs of the program and our own observations and knowledge. (This point of view corresponds to the presently dominant attitude towards the foundations of mathematics. We study the structure of mathematical systems — from the outside as it were — using whatever metamathematical tools seem useful, instead of assuming as little as possible and building up axiom by axiom and rule by rule within a system.)"

The quotation is an excellent explanation why we find it important to underline the historical continuity and revolutionary novelty of the problems treated here. *Havel,* the brother of the excellent playwright and present president of Czechoslovakia, summarized these and several similar considerations by the comment: *Artificial Intelligence is applied epistemology* [Havel 1985].

> "The hypotheses are scaffoldings which are built in constructing but as the edifice is ready we pull down. They are indispensable for the worker but it is essential that we should not consider the scaffolding as the building."
>
> *Goethe: Maxims and Reflections*

Chapter 1
Models and Representations

1.1 Models — science — reality

In this book we shall speak about the *instruments of model building,* a discipline of computer representation. Models were built well before computers. Any abstraction, verbal or mathematical, which attempted to describe the world or some distinct part of it were modellings from this point of view. They are used for finding relations among events, transmitting knowledge to others, and forecasting future events. We should not add such attributes as naive or scientific, because models are representations created by the human brain, i.e. by a double reflection: the reflection of the world in the brain and the reflection of this brain picture in the communication media by spoken and written words, figures, formulas, etc. This reflection-representation is dependent on the status of its media, i.e. it cannot have any absolute measure of validity. Most philosophers of science nowadays express these lessons as the principle of socio-historical relativity of science: What is accepted as scientific truth, or a correct way of reasoning, is dependent on the conventions of the dominant scientific community of the period. We can admit this relativity in view of our considerations with a slight caution that is a direct consequence of our modelling faculty: A model (i.e. a theory, a calculus)* can be correct if it works to some extent, if it has some predictive power for some future event (experiment, effect, phenomenon).

Models are used for explanation as well as for prediction. The explanation feature is, nevertheless, nearer to beliefs, and the predictive to experience, although the two are often mixed, in both superstitious notions and scientific theories.

The primitive models of weather used by some tribal peoples were correct by this standard, although the explanation sometimes involved spiritual beings. *Pythagoras* mixed his ingenious and still valid ideas on geometry and numbers with very confused mystic ones; as *Bertrand Russell* [1945] once commented, he could have been a mixture of an *Einstein* and a *Mary Baker Eddy*, founder of Christian Science. What might be said about our own scientific models in 4500 A.D.? The Ptolemaic model of the solar system worked well for about one and a half millennia. Science sometimes consciously uses artificial, unrealistic models such as, e.g. the demon dreamed up by Maxwell.

A model will become obsolate if it is replaced by a new one that covers more predictable phenomena and leaves fewer that are contrary to its conclusions. *Karl Popper*'s [1963] strong principle of a refutation model combined with a positive model of conjecture can be used only in very simple, theoretical cases. We will come back to this point later, be-

---

* Referring to the nomenclature, see the comment at the end of this section.

cause it is a main topic of our considerations. We mention here only that the resolution principle [Robinson 1965] used for the proof of correctness of computer programs—which is a practical realization of the refutation principle in a logically well-described, closed model—is not useful in realistic cases. Later, in Section 3.1 we shall see how ancient this epistemic method really is.

No *absolute measure exists* for the final judgement on the validity of a model. *God, whether one believes in Him or not, is the finest model of model assessment: a Being who knows everything simultaneously, in every dimension, in infinite space and infinite time.* Validity can be perfectly provable only if a model works in every condition, i.e. only if it is true and provides true conclusions in every circumstance. If we take this point, then we shall not become lost in the apparent inadequacies of models: A good car engineer can use his car very efficiently with knowledge of its limitations, possible failures and also knowing that this knowledge is not complete by far in covering all the possible events that could occur as the mechanism is used.

This candor about our knowledge is needed, and it is a relevant part of knowledge—it functions as a soft, humanistic version of the conjecture and refutation requirement. It can be argued at length whether this process of model review (a research program in *Lakatos'* [1963, 1970] sense) is a convergent one or not. Convergence in this sense could be the meaning of the concept of model development. My opinion is that this also belongs to the God class of problem, i.e. it can be estimated in a final sense only from omniscience. If we take the continuous process of having evermore general models used for more accurate prediction of a greater number of events, then there would be no doubt (or at least much less doubt) of a convergence—assuming we are not worried by the infinite length of this process. As we find more and more new problems which are related to certain well-detectable limits of our modelling abilities, we start to be more skeptical on the certainty of convergence than our ancestors in the beautifully optimistic Age of Reason. In this century we have met several basic problems of mankind in economics, social coexistence, relationship to nature, biology, and technology which suggest that they too are beyond our present model building skills. We have lost the certainty of such a convergence that can lead to real solutions.

We do not even know whether our intellectual abilities set a limit in principle to cognition. The dog's brain can never understand *Maxwell*'s equations. The existence of a similar but, of course, higher limit—still below the real relationships governing Nature—could, hypothetically, create a distorted convergence.

These remarks are also made in a soft way: *We have no overall model of our model building abilities* as well! This is why we cannot offer any last word on the convergence of models to a final truth.

Lastly, a minor remark on nomenclature. Model, theory, calculus have slightly different interpretations by various authors and in different disciplines. We use the word "model" similarly for a mental representation, for a verbal description, and for a logico-mathematical formularization. This usage emphasizes the representation features versus the Reality; let us hope that it does not cause any confusion. In this context, "theory" can be seen as a metamodel, a generalization of models, and "calculus" as the procedures used in the computations of models.

1.2 Complexity is the key

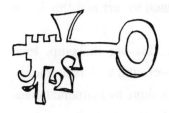 The kernel of all problems seems to lie in complexity. Complexity has been with mankind from the very beginning. But this was not realized until man created for himself an artificial environment that went beyond the models used in its creation. The apocryphal question of God's ability to create a stone which He cannot lift became a question for man as well.

While nature alone manifested the complexity, it was somehow hidden by the umbrella of transcendental concepts. The long struggle of thinkers to implant the concepts of God into a rationalistic human conceptual frame is a sign of this process. As people discovered that we can create a complexity beyond the limits of comprehension, we began to take a new look at the problem. We can meditate on the causality or at least historical synchronism of this technological-economic-social outgrowth with developments in mathematics. Various theoretical structures exhibited similar problems and ultimately led to revolutionary revisions of the concepts of truth and general validity. It should be enough to state that the maturing of an intellectual attitude is an extremely complex process, with many unclear interrelationships. Much could be written and demonstrated on very similar trends in modern arts as all traditional structures and values were dissolved. Analogously to the quest for elementary particles and basic forces in physics, fundamentals appeared in the arts: An exploration of the most simple forms and colours (e.g. *Mondrian, Malewitch, Moholy Nagy, Rothko*), of the origins of harmony (e.g. *Schönberg*) or words (e.g. *Apollinaire*) and the resulting confusion after finding that those final elements do not reveal the key to totality (e.g. *Kandinsky, Pollock*, the Dada, *John Cage* and the whole modern music of noise). *"The hidden face of Nature"* [Kállai 1947] was the title of an essay on these trends of modern art and this is the real mirror of the Zeitgeist.*

We must have a realistic candor after this big shake-up, look around where we are now, without the usual over- and understatements. Complexity is the keyword. Thanks to the work done by mathematicians in complexity theory and especially in algorithmic complexity, we have clear distinctions of complexity levels and thus estimates for computability, i.e. for the applicability of models [Hopcroft and Ullman 1979; Harel 1987].

In order to arrive at the level of computational complexity, i.e. to our present problems, which are well discussed at best, we return now to the phases of representations, reflections.

The first three phases of reflections within the modelling process were well-known to the philosophers of the Stoa. They were quoted by Sextus about 500 years later: "The Stoics say that three things are linked together, that which is signified, that which signifies and the object." As we stated in the introduction, a fourth phase of reflection is present. The reflection by the sensory system, this one by the brain, and the brain's reflection, reflected in media, is now reflected—represented—in computers. The first question would be if this is really a fourth reflection, i.e. is it different from those which were given in a written form before? The answer is a clear 'yes', and behind that lies an important paradox which points to the dangers of computer representation. The computer model

---

* "The taste and outlook characteristic of a period or generation" – The American Heritage Dictionary

is simultaneously much more powerful than those which have been used till now, and less powerful as well. The positive side is apparent and therefore misleading: The computer handles more data, more calculation steps, by many orders of magnitude than any model before, i.e. it can be much richer in considering relations between parameters. The negative is hidden in the transfer problems of multimedia information (natural language, pictures, metacommunication, etc.) into the relatively narrow band instruments of algorithms and programs. Consciously or unconsciously several simplifications, omissions are committed by this process; an expert at modelling and programming does this in a way similar to trained interpreters. They automatically transform the text to the idioms, the ways of thinking of the other culture.

The next stage is computation itself. A model described correctly by a partial differential equation or an elliptic integro-differential equation goes over an iterative approximation procedure which is taken by the programmer from a library. Anybody who has used these methods, knows that it is always risky to predict how correct the resulting data will be at certain circumstances (e.g. boundary conditions). Finally, we have the psychological illusion of computers previously mentioned: After all these simplifications, transformations, omissions and truncating, people have the misleading belief that this answer should be objective, true because it has been generated by a computer. This is why we emphasize the point that computer representation is a fourth reflection of reality, containing all the problems of the first three and adding new dimensions to them.

The complexity measure generally used is, therefore, restricted to computational complexity. It reflects, however, the much broader range of complexity—just as with the four levels of reflection, this is the *computational representation* of complexity. Taking a system containing

N discrete components, computational needs and computational complexity are low if the problem related to the interaction of these components can be solved in N or $NlogN$ steps. The problem is more complex if the computational time demanded for the solution grows by powers of N. The problem solution is then called polynomial. Problems for which the computational demand grows exponentially with N and faster, are practically unsolvable, if N is not trivially small. A 2^N type problem with $N=100$ requires about 2000 times more time on a giga-flops speed supercomputer than the supposed life of the Universe, an N^N type one with $N=20$ only needs about two hundred times more than our time after the Big Bang. *NP complete* problems apparently behave this way and several practical problems, e.g. linear programming, belong to this class. Many ordering problems are proven to be NP hard, i.e. proven unsolvable in an exact way for a relatively low number of components. How to manage these problems of combinatorial explosion is an open, and, at present, highly challenging task of mathematics. These investigations indicate that complexity has a similar fine structure as the related concept of infinity: Convergence and reliability of approximations, orders of magnitude, practical and theoretical limits are now a focus of research. As infinite sets have different cardinality, computational complexity and problems beyond computational modelling have the same hierarchy. Some algorithms, e.g. have a hyperexponential time requirement. We see now really hard limits and these deeply concern the computational aspect of the modelling procedure. The picture becomes even worse if the problem is not continuous. Discretization raises questions, continuity and nonlinearity appear. We can never take into consideration all those extremely relevant parameters, interactions beyond the one-to-one computational mapping of mathematical models.

The *Skolem-Löwenheim theorem*, as the counterpart of *Gödel's incompleteness theorem*, indicates that these indefinite limits do not refer only to intentional, mental states, or psychological phenomena. *Gödel* proved that a set of axioms (a model, in our sense) is not adequate to prove all the theorems belonging to this model; the descending Skolem-Löwenheim theorem proves that a model (a set of axioms, precisely a theory over a countable language*) has at least a countably infinite representation. Not only mental but also mathematical models have no definite, finite borders!

Myhill [1951] argues about the philosophical consequences of the Skolem-Löwenheim theorem. He concludes it has none, because this theorem relates only to formal systems and proves only the poverty of formal systems in enforcing limits to their subject. This is just the conclusion we can use for our computer epistemology! Computer knowledge is, and, as far as our perspective reaches will be, a kind of a formal system, if memory, the speed of processing, and parallelism are developed to any extent.

A new perspective is opened possibly by a brand new result in theoretical computer science. At the end of the last year a group of young computer scientists in Chicago and Tel Aviv (*A. Shamir, C. Lund, H. Karloff, N. Nisan, L. Fortnow*) found an efficient protocol for verifying theorems about models of extremely high complexity. In this framework two agents, the prover (also called Merlin)** and a verifier (also called

---

* See the last remark of Section 1.1.
** The names of the Arthurian legend are borrowed by *L. Babai* who used to be a professor of this group. An example for NP problems is a special ordering task of the knights around the Round Table if the number of the knights highly exceeds that of legend (say 150) [Babai 1990].

Arthur) cooperate to present convincing probabilistic evidence on the truth of a theorem. Merlin has infinite computing powers, Arthur has only limited resources (i.e. he is impatient) but accepts statistical evidence. Merlin can be thought of as a theorem generator on a supercomputer, while Arthur as a machine with modest computing capabilities. The theorem generator by some highly sophisticated algorithm can simulate the intuitive heuristic of the human, not in a logical way as those we shall speak about in Chapter 5. This latter possibility is not yet proved, but stimulates new aspects of this relevant issue.

The class of problems admitting interactive proofs in this sense (and this is the new result) is *PSPACE*. A problem belongs to *PSPACE* if it can be solved using a polynomial amount of workspace. *PSPACE* is widely believed to contain problems much more difficult than those in *NP*.

Two interesting issues should be mentioned which are related to the subject of computer epistemology. The first is this new man-machine interaction: intuitive problem formulation (model creation) by human or computer-aided human intuition and computer verification by a limited certainty. The other was the way of distribution and fast further development of this result: The group has sent electronic mail about the new finding and received a cooperation between Chicago and Tel Aviv by the same computer network media. Until now no publication could follow this 'good news' — in ancient Greek euangelion. This reminds us of the exchange of scientific ideas by letter, used mostly between the 17th and 19th centuries but in a nearly real time process and in our extended global intellectual community! The relevance of all these can hardly be underestimated.

And finally a slightly disappointing remark — to see the pros and cons everywhere: All those results above can be used only if we (Arthur) have a well-formulated model of the problem but we are just discussing the weaknesses and limits of this mathematical or verbal model building capability!

1.3 Epistemic constituents of model complexity

Let us make a short preliminary review of different (mostly superimposed) reasons for model complexity (the second and third reflections).

The first and most obvious reason is the number of interactions. Even if the system is linear and the behavior is stationary, but neither the components nor the interactions are identical, the matrix of interaction is not sparse. We need to get into the details of this trivial but computationally lengthy problem – passing it with a sarcastic, melancholic remark that this was and still is realized by the bloody dictators of our century: To execute their paranoid ideas about order, they tried to put everybody in a uniform straitjacket. All who seemed not to volunteer have been annihilated, to get a uniform society matrix of zero nondiagonal components.

The second explosive issue of complexity is the probability-uncertainty bundle. This is the subject of Chapter 2.

The third is related to nonlinearity and a special consequence of that, chaotic behavior. We refer here to the tremendous and excellent literature on that subject.*

The fourth source of explosion is rooted in logic and language, in the uncertainties of reasoning due to the meaning problem and the related communication uncertainties. This will be the topic of Chapters 3 and 4.

We can ask if this partition is complete and correct. There is no definite answer to this question. We must return to the God's-eye view idea. He could be the only being who could judge if relationships among those conceptual items which point towards the unknown are well-interpreted or not. In our earthly view these phenomena appear mostly as lacking some kind of structure. Can we classify the nature of everything with the above classes of uncertainty, i.e. create an exact topography and natural history of the unexplored? These are somewhat different formulations of the same eternal question of epistemology. Let us accept the above classifications as practical conventions for our further discussions.

---

* [Poincaré 1892; Neumann 1963; Mandelbrot 1977; Hao Bai-Lin 1984; Gleick 1987]

Chapter 2
Uncertainty — probability
— Preliminary warning and apology —

In this section, and later in the chapter, we get into a contradiction of the subject and our approach — which reveals the weakness of the latter: We shall speak in a bit more detail about similarities and divergencies of the uncertainty methods, about their epistemic background and relations to practical usage, returning to the most characteristic methods from different aspects several times. This will be done in a superficial, sketchy way; otherwise we would have to write a full textbook chapter on different methods of uncertainty. For those who are not familiar with these methods, I tried to give a short summary in the Appendix but the reader is advised to consult the recommended readings and the quoted literature to get more authentic information. The Appendix is organized in a sequence which gets increasingly further from probabilistic orthodoxy, and this succession is mostly followed in the main text as well. This relates to the following set:

- probabilistic reasoning [Nilsson 1986]—Appendix 1
- Bayesian methods [Pearl 1988]—Appendix 2
- Dempster-Shafer method [Shafer 1976]—Appendix 3
- certainty factor procedures [Buchanan-Shortliffe 1984]
  —Appendix 4
- possibilistic-fuzzy methods [Zadeh 1965, 1968;
  Dubois and Prade 1988]—Appendix 5
- endorsement [Cohen 1985]—Appendix 6.

Readers not too much interested in details of the different methods are advised to skim those, especially Sections 2.7 and 2.8.

2.1 An uncertain historical retrospection

Few topics have as vast a professional literature, written by the most scholarly authors, as do probability and uncertainty. I refer here to *Kolmogorov* [1933, 1965] and *Carnap* [1950]. I really hesitated, uncertain that I could add anything to all this, not being a real expert in either mathematics or in philosophy. The drive to do so came from my own practical experience as we started to apply these concepts in AI. This was just the factual encounter with the direct feedback effect of the representation vs. reality problem. We can understand why probability-uncertainty was the last development of philosophy and is as uncertain as it has been till now—and may continue to be for ever. Ancient and some present-day people regarded events as distributed into two distinct classes. Those which could be influenced by human action were the focus of scientific, analytical interest [David 1962]. All others which happened irregularly, in an indetectable way, and/or which could not be influenced by man were attributed to anthropomorphic superhuman powers. This view is best reflected in the Greek tragedies of destiny. Later developments, also begun by the ancient Greek philosophers, attributed a transcendental superhuman logic or quasi-geometric planning to God. The only major topic of discussion was the question of whether this transcendental logic can or cannot be known by man. Should such an endeavor be regarded as a sacrilege or as a blessed search for the Divine Truth?

One of the most characteristic pictures of this world-view (Weltanschauung) is given by its contrast. The atheist *Lucretius* quickly reached a conclusion surprisingly similar to the recent one of physics.

> "Not with design or reasoning shrewd did all
> The first beginnings take their divers posts
> Each in his proper place; nor yet, forsooth,
> Did they by mutual compact fix upon
> Their several movements; but in numbers vast
> Shifting now here, now there, throughout the Whole,
> Harried by blows relentless down the course
> Of endless time, trying now this, now that
> Of motion and of union, they at last
> Came into patterns such as those whereby
> This world of ours is built, and standeth fast."

Lucretius: On the Nature of Things
(de Rerum Natura), transl. Ch. E. Bennett
Walter J. Black, Roslyn, NY, 1946

He differs from most later deists and atheists in not substituting a Rational Law, Human Mind, etc., for God in whole or in part, because science and general knowledge had not reached the level of later ages when this hope looked to be justified.

We see that probability in a modern sense hardly existed. Everything which is surprising, unknown, was supposed to be a deterministic, definite consequence of the Higher Action. The more primitive, but in some sense more up-to-date, myth includes an actually existing probability in the emotional behavior of the Gods (remember the Lord of the Old Testament, merciful and vengeful—Exodus, 34, or the envy of the Greek Gods), in a similar fashion to the Maxwell's-demon metaphor. The more advanced, monotheistic belief does not acknowledge anything finally uncertain. The Age of Reason's ways of thinking were inherently deterministic. Probability was restricted to games, not events of Nature. The reasons behind uncertain events were supposed to act either according to the earlier paradigm or by a hypothesis of countless small interactions. The history of these philosophical developments runs parallel to the uncertainty problem in the natural sciences. The main issue until now has been this: If uncertainty is a real form of existence of Nature or is a human model, is it a reflection of the limits of human knowledge, or is there, behind apparently random events, a firm law, or rather a universal system of a law-like construct ruling the world? Is it epistemic or ontological in the vernacular of philosophy?

Modern physics first began the progress of rationalist scientific thinking towards an ideal of a construct of coherent laws of nature which can evolve to be a general key for every problem. In this respect, about a century ago statistical thermodynamics played an ambiguous role: It introduced random processes into the converging world of *Newton, Euler, Lagrange, Gauss, Hamilton, Maxwell* and others, who created even more general mathematical models of the world's dynamics. This new, statistical model was really powerful and promising, it had just that feature of a model which is the most relevant justification of their validity: It could be used for prediction of events, helping people to design new devices, using paper and pencil and finding that the devices behaved in good correspondence with the ideas of the designer. The computer seemed the last step in completing this process, a giant lever of design for all those problems that seemed clear theoretically but whose calculation, as prescribed by the model, was excessively cumbersome. Statistical thermodynamics broke this line because it acknowledged the randomness of Brownian motion—just such motion was the focus of computable models and the basic paradigm of all model constructs—but it could extend the basic models in a marvelous harmony by explaining several phenomena and providing new calculational instruments. Mechanics, thermal phenomena, and energy in its different forms could be associated in more general models than previously, and these models also could be used in particle physics or nuclear reactors, where design was based on thermodynamical models. The model could be extended—its most transcendental concept, entropy, could be related to information theory.

Further developments in modern physics that changed traditional views and concepts of rational thinking are discussed much better in many sources; we mention only that the desire for a computable world order was a prevalent idea in human thinking. Identifying the idea of God with a Great Geometer was seen first in the thinking of some Greek philosophers progressing towards the monotheist view of a Unified Order, but this trend was strengthened through the Middle Ages, the Age of Reason, until *Einstein* stated his famous argument

against the uncertainty interpretation of quantum theory: That God does not play dice. ("Der Hergott würfelt nicht.")

The relationship of computation and physics reflects our basic problems. One aspect is the problem of measurement, i.e. a well-defined, executable program for a measurement to a defined accuracy, e.g. how to measure the relation of the diameter and circumference of a circle, or how to measure quantum numbers. Another is computation, a well-defined computer program which calculates physical numbers (e.g. those above) and halts at a certain defined approximation. Physics found that there is not yet a complete and satisfactory one-to-one correspondence between the two [Geroch and Hartle 1986]. This would not effect relevant practical consequences; doubts start with such facts as the physical reality is diverging due to small differences. This is typical for chaotic processes—the widely quoted *Butterfly Effect* (a butterfly beating its wings in Beijing can evoke turbulences which could be amplified, later causing a disastrous storm in New York) but also in the world of elementary particles due to ultimately unknown behaviors.

The role of "small" deviations causing "large" effects hints at the problem to be discussed in Sections 5.9 and 5.12 in another aspect—cognition. But these relations of cognition have a factual basis in the different dimensions of the Reality. We are uncertain about the real *metric of the event spaces* because we perceive, measure, compute, define these metrics always from the point of view (here we use the geometric-physical metaphor) of some particular certain projections within the limited space-frame of an unexplored and unlimited higher dimension. This metaphor looks to be a valid interpretation of all relativities discussed later concerning logic, concepts, etc. The contradictions of metrics are all due to the relativity of a prejudicial lower dimensional view working within its partly unknown limits. But if circumstances shift to another view, the other dimensions previously neglected become relevant. This interpretation is misleadingly beautiful—another reflection of the structure of Reality in our mind! It remains workable within the same limits as other structures interpreted by the mind. The sequence of mirror images is unlimited but in some sense—as we will see when we return to these ideas in Section 5.12—it is a realistic development of mirrors!

Why, in encountering computer intelligence, do we meet the same partly consolidated, partly open problems of science renewed? We have to see the critical importance of the input to a calculation process that provides a solution according to a model where we have no real control over this calculation procedure.

This is the reason why we try to separate the problem into the four distinct reflections, representations, each one having its own speciality of qualification. Obviously we bother less with the basic philosophical part of the problem: What kind of laws or ultimate Will governs the world? We look more into the questions of the further mapping relations. Our main concern relates to our existing models of those phenomena that contain relevant uncertainties for us. That is, they can be uncertain because they are created and exist having these uncertainties inherently, as their nature. Alternatively, these uncertainties can be due to our limited general knowledge of their relationships or limitations resulting from other circumstances of observation. The latter reflection comes closer to computational methods, their requirements, and inference considerations.

2.2 Inadequacy of the classical model

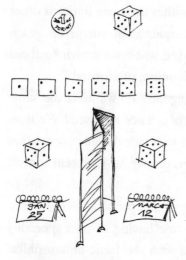

The theory of probability formulated by *Kolmogorov* [1933] is based on event algebra and measure theory. I think that this approach is a useful one for the entire problem if we take it as a general model of events which can have different interpretations or hypothetical conditions. In that way it can be a meta-model for all events, consequences, whose estimates are to some extent uncertain. As emphasized, for our models (computer models) it is totally irrelevant – from this point of view only – whether uncertainty is an inherent feature of the phenomena, i.e. it is ontological or only due to momentary or generic lack of knowledge and would be certain from God's eye (epistemic).

The doubts of those who tried to escape from the rigor of probability calculus was about the hypothesis of the initial model.

The original model was based on coin or dice throwing, i.e. events where:

A. Each event is *independent* from the others (including previous ones).

B. The outcomes of these events can be classified into a *known number of cases* (as heads or tails, or 1-6 faces on a die). We could include the principle of excluded middle in this condition. If a predicate on something is not true, it must be false, and vice versa. This means that all assumptions are valid only if the classification is complete, invariant against any time or other conditions, and crisply delimited.

C. The number of outcomes is *quasimonotonous* in each of the cases of condition B. After a certain number of events (experiments) there is a convergence relationship among the sum of the events and the number of events classified in the above cases. This implies the convergence of statistical characteristics (distribution, etc.) after a certain "high" number of samplings. The situation of complete certainty is reached only by observation of an infinite number of events (God's eye).

D. *No* circumstance influencing the events *changes* in any way during the observation (an ideal of perfection, like eternity in Heaven).

Nobody working with uncertain events was so naive as to not consider these absolute limitations. Nevertheless this model worked in a great number of extremely important cases where the limit of quasimonotonicity could be reached and other circumstances approximated the ideal model. This was not only the case in the original models, but also in thermodynamics, the behavior of elementary particles, some characteristics of large human populations, etc.

The extreme criticism of the probability approach was based on the idea that any probability measure contains some prejudices about the behavior of the phenomenon, e.g. those ones which were enumerated before. There are several others, such as the hypothesis of an unbiased, symmetrical estimate, or the supposition of certain distribution models. The latter worked quite impressively in the different statistics of thermodynamics (as e.g. *Boltzmann*'s, *Bose-Einstein*'s or *Maxwell*'s) [Feynman, Leighton and Sands 1963]. Nevertheless this criticism and the successes of probability in several applications indicate the core of the problem and its possible treatment. In every case we have to go back to the model of the events, take this as a hypothesis and look carefully at the limitations of validity.

The weakening of the above conditions could also be done by an extension of the conceptual model for those weak conditions, using the calculus itself (confidence intervals, reliability estimates, probability propagations of different influencing conditions, etc.) These extensions are all deeply related to the epistemic background, dependent on the hypothetical model related to the extension. They can be very helpful, sometimes the only way of calculation, but should be taken with much salt and pepper!

The relationship of statistics and probability are also disputed. We quote here *Savage* [1954]: "It is unanimously agreed that statistics depend somehow on probability. But, as to what probability is and how it is connected with statistics, there has seldom been such complete disagreement and breakdown of communication since the Tower of Babel. There must be dozens of different interpretations of probability defended by living authorities, and some authorities hold that several different interpretations may be useful, that is, that the concept of probability may have different meaningful senses in different contexts. Doubtless, much of the disagreement is merely terminological and would all disappear under sufficiently sharp analysis. Some believe that it would all disappear, or even that they have themselves already made the necessary analysis."

2.3 The first mapping — measurement and uncertainty

 For our purposes, statistics is related to measurements and methods of evaluation of measurements, probability, and uncertainty of predictions based either on statistics or on model considerations. The measurement problem as a computer input has been sometimes neglected until now, since the impressive abilities of computers conceal the uncertain knowledge about the nature of the inputs. It was long argued that all the delicacies of modern physics relate to the world of elementary particles and cosmogony, i.e. just those spheres that have not too much in common with our realistic everyday problems. Events of the microworld, though uncertain in their incomprehensible dimensions, compose a more or less easily treatable conglomerate for applying statistics or measurements in macro. However, it turned out that this reasoning is valid only if the interactions are simple, rather uniform, under those special conditions where the law of large numbers works.

The quandaries arise everywhere in the macroworld of practical applications as well. Everyone who has had the task in process control of measuring physical and chemical parameters found the same doubts about what we do: e.g. flow measurement in a noncircular gas duct, estimating furnace temperatures, continuous estimating of raw material composition,etc. The same problems and even more intricate ones occur in bioengineering, economics, or any other control task at this point, in a manner that is independent from the dynamics of the process. As indicated previously, speaking on certainty in measurement, this is not a clear-cut issue.

Every measurement and especially those related to statistics conceals a certain model hypothesis, i.e. a predictive element, that, with some slight malevolence, can also be called a prejudice. The method of measurement and its physical implementation are mostly based on some model-hypotheses, in several cases on just the same model which would be parametrized by the measurement. This is one reason only why we have to add to the relativity of models another, seemingly softer component: subjectivity, or intuition, judgement, creativity, prejudice, ignorance, and the narrow-mindedness of the people who are involved. Once more a problem of the model: how the events, the phenomena are reflected, classified, and structured in the minds of the people concerned. If we accept this view and can accustom ourselves to it, then all combatant groups and terminologies can be reconciled and we can dig deeper in the bottomless well of Reality. Nevertheless, we find some useful resources more frequently!

2.4 Statistics and uncertainty

The two basic deviations, according to *Shafer* [1987b], are the frequentist and the Bayesian-subjective approaches. The frequentist view should be the objective one, a statistics based on all data relevant to the phenomenon. As we can easily recognize, this is also a hypothesis-laden condition in any case where the definitions are more complex and therefore more ambiguous than that of a coin or a dice; e.g. observation of passenger traffic which is almost as clear-cut as those archetypal cases, needs limit definitions on height, age, passenger, and serviceman etc., all dependent on the objective of the statistical analysis, such as whether the analysis is done for frequency scheduling or tariff planning, for example. Any further analysis requires coincidences of those classification data with season, hour of the day, district, etc.

Practically no (or at least very few) statistical analyses can be made without considering the objective of observation and that introduces subjective classification procedures, i.e. the transflux of the Bayesian-subjective impurities into an ideal, uncorrupted view of frequency registration. The Bayesian approach covers a clearly subjective component: We group the data into classes which are hypothetical distinctions, the definition of the classes incorporates our view of the structure of the phenomenon, which is just what we would like to explore by observation! Anybody can argue that this is fine, exactly the right and usual way of scientific research: Starting with a zero approximation one can iterate by observing the differences of the hypotheses and of the phenomena and in this way an iterative approximation can be reached both in data and in the theory (hypotheses). This is true if the convergence is granted for the data themselves and for the hypothesis (i.e. for the concluding theory). A warning of most relevant discoveries speaks against any automatic assumption of this convergence. Even the convergence itself can be misleading: It can assert a phenomenon which is a demonstration of a false hypothesis. This happens frequently in medical practice or in social phenomena. Remember the Winnie-the-Pooh effect: tracing one's own steps!

The classification problem is much deeper. One issue, agreed to rather easily by both statistical orthodoxy and neology, is a distinction between the unknown and the unexplored. We referred to the ancient idea of the excluded middle, the view that something can be classified in

one specific class and the statement of that classification is true if this
something belongs to the class or false if not. The binary distinction of
true and false can only be accepted either as an extreme simplification
in really simple cases (simple is also a relative concept depending on the
objective, the subject, and the circumstances), or as a pragmatic way of
problem solving in cases where we are aware of the concerns ultimately,
or from God's eye, for a holistic, ideal view of every possibility. For the
Bayesian conceptualization, the unexplored is a region of conditions
where we have no (or no satisfactory) statistics but where we can define
these conditional cases well, leaving no region out of consideration, and
the number of conditions can be fixed (as in the case of dice). On May
4, 1493, Rodrigo de Borgia, as Pope *Alexander VI*, divided the unexplored globe in that way between Spain and Portugal in his bull: Inter
Caetera Divini (Among Other Divine!). The unknown is an undefined region where we do not have an estimate how many possibilities exist, how
they are related or nonrelated to the known classes. On late maps large
regions of present Russia were indicated in that way, noted as: ubi leones
sunt (where lions are living) or, as on some 18th Century American
maps: extensive meadows full of buffalos.

In this manner statistical analysis, which looked to be an exact, unbiased, objective measure backed by a firm theory of sampling, confidence, and distribution, was softened. By these sideways steps, settling
on relevant characteristics further softens the procedure, granting a
nearly equal role to subjective impressions on estimates, coined as *guess*,
belief, Certainty Factor, evidence, or *subjective probability*. We have to
notice that statistics and beliefs are not exactly separated. We smuggle,
consciously or unconsciously, subjective elements into statistics and, subjective estimates contain always some kind of statistical observations. A
professional practice is more or less a statistical analysis of the profes-

sion over the statistics of professional individuals, although, as we shall refer to later as well, human subjective statistics are extremely biased. In other words, we call this kind of statistics—heavily criticized in Chapter 5—professional skill, knowledge, or expertise. It is also evident that in most cases, a better estimate can be made if we have a clear picture of all possible cases but no available data on some of them (the unexplored) than in a situation where we encounter an unknown set of unknown cases with no knowledge of the influence of those on the known (the unknown). This difference was demonstrated earlier by the metaphor of having a topography of an area but no details on some regions. The Dempster-Shafer theory undertook to put these unclear regions into the framework of usual methods and because it was done with no essential offence against them, the liberal wing of statistical orthodoxy accepted it. The different natures of uncertainty to be discussed later in Section 2.6—e.g. if a hypothesis has a certain probability or the provability is guessed to be uncertain to some extent—play an important role in the formulation of the methods and interpretations but they get a common framework in calculations. *Pearl,* basing his work on the Bayesian model, *Dubois* and *Prade* on the possibilistic approach, *Kyburg,* from a more philosophical point of view, did a lot to illustrate this common framework.

We have to mention that this leads away from the condition of *equal chances* for distinct cases, although it was not completely abandoned in estimations on unknown regions. The equal chance (as is obvious in looking at the archetype) is a reduction to first principles, the basic binary choice of true and false. If we encounter any phenomena that do not obey the principle of equal chance, then we endeavor to find some causal relation behind the uneven distribution until we reach a final one of equal chance. Is there any? A trivial example would be the random walk over the prime numbers. Each interval has a different chance but no general algorithm is found to generate them, i.e. no rule of scaling for an equal chance. Some modern methods of statistics are aware of this phenomenon and attempt to use it (jackknife, bootstrapping) but they cannot avoid some previous or self-generated bias-pitfalls. Here and anywhere in cases of phenomena irreducible to these hypothetical binary primitives, we find the infinite dark wells of uncertainties in human ways of reasoning. This is another aspect of the God's-eye view!

Being as weak as we are, we use the set model and the event algebra for these set models which offer a rather noncontroversial judgement for the treatment of different situations which are the consequences of the heterogeneous nature of available data.

2.5 Subjective knowledge—fuzziness

 The recognition of the need for handling subjective information in the framework of statistics and probability led to the introduction, and thus to the controversies of fuzzy concepts. As everything, this has several antecedents. We mention here only *Max Black*'s 1937 paper with some references to earlier ideas. Speaking of these different views and nomenclatures (something is also an issue of argumentation if it is only another view or another nomenclature), the words probability and uncertainty are used equally, sometimes in the same sense, sometimes in distinct ones. In this essay we try to apply *probability* in the more traditional sense (although it has been shown that this sense has more or less orthodox and liberal wings as well) and use *uncertainty* for

the whole issue, comprising those dark regions of conjectures, beliefs, prejudices, or not well-defined concepts, and, unfortunately, most of the real world. The *fuzzy idea* is a natural consequence of this reality, stemming from two adjoining necessities. The first and original necessity is strongly related to computers and expert systems: a need for translating subjective verbal judgements into digital data. The problem is clarified by the following simple example:

Let us have a statement: "If the boy is smaller than Mary, then she does not dance with him"; and another: "Joe is smaller than Mary". This will be a purely logical task, with no transfer of attributes to a numerical form needed. The other simple version: Mary is 5'7", Joe is 5'5". Again, there is no need for transformation from the numerical to conceptual. If we say that Mary is tall for her age and sex, and that Joe is an adult of medium size, the problem is uncertain and, if we do not want to get involved in combinatorial tables indicating all possible cases of height related to or belonging to a sex, having a certain age, etc. (a similar procedure would be if we had a complete multiplication table instead of a multiplication algorithm), we would have to do some transfers from these uncertain attributes to numerical data. We should not forget the role of tacit knowledge: The same attributes of height have different meanings in Sweden or in Southern Italy, the age and growth relationships are also different. We might have in mind a hint about the usual height of heels related to the occasion, the year's fashion, and Mary's preferences. We see that in some estimates we can use regular statistics, e.g. the average heights of girls, aged 16, black, in the state of Illinois, but some are very subjective. They have no relation with any direct statistics, no confidence measures for them can be defined.

The arguments of the liberal interpretation of probability are well accepted: If the idea of subjective probability is agreed to, everything can be expressed by belief, uncertainty, and evidence measures. A hypothetical distribution (i.e. a subjective measure of the strength of the belief) can also be attributed, and the fuzzy relations are merged into a subjective probability.

The other distinction made by the fuzzy nomenclature relates to a relativistic view: The original probability concepts are related to fixed measures (the side of the dice, the height of the girl etc.) and the events are uncertain. The fuzzy idea is more aligned to the opposite circumstance: The events can be certain (Mary's height is an exact value) but the system of coordinates, of measures, is uncertain (if it is high in those respects). The relationship of the two views is dualistic, i.e. the results are not different, the nomenclature indicates the difference of views and this is not irrelevant as we analyze the pitfalls of a computer representation against the real world. We encounter here another aspect of the metric problem of Sections 2.1, 5.2, 5.11—we cannot even define whether the uncertainty of the data or the uncertainty of the metric should be considered as the static or the dynamic feature of the uncertainty phenomenon.

The fuzzy view is a way of thinking that tries to resolve the problem of sharp but uncertain concepts. We come back to this in Section 4.5. Here we only quote *Noam Chomsky*: "Philosophers often take perfectly sensible continua and get in trouble by trying to convert them into dichotomics."

Another important aspect of the fuzzy method is the transfer of verbal communication into computer input, i.e. numerical estimates. Cognitive psychology has very contradictory experimental results on the reliability and the repeatability of these mappings.* A well-disciplined

---

* [Cliff 1959; Kahneman and Tversky 1972; Zimmer 1984; Doyle 1988]

use of the fuzzy method can help in improving these unavoidable mapping distortions.

The uncertainty about uncertainty and the fusion of instruments and ideas is nicely demonstrated by the proposal for the *endorsement* method [Cohen 1985]. This is an attempt to avoid all numerical games on probability estimates and create a real, proper, rule-based artificial intelligence system. It collects all confirmatory and refuting statements, similar to a ledger book of assets and debts, and arranges these into a rule system for endorsing or weakening a hypothesis. Nevertheless, all judgements must have a decision rule weighing the pros and cons, each compared against the others. In that way the whole concept is a brief detour from probability-uncertainty through logic to the patterns of Chapter 5, bypassing the ultimate problem of metric (Section 5.9). Unfortunately this bypass is not a substitute for any solution. Ostrich policies denying the problem do not help in the uncertainty desert either. Not by chance, the proposal has not had many adherents until now, and the examples given by the author are so simple that they can be easily surveyed by human judgement.

As we see most ideologies do not show much difference in the assignment of basic uncertainty values to predicates, only the interpretations and the nomenclature varies. In order to check a model's relationship to reality in these respects we must scrutinize the interpretation semantics and its further consequences.

2.6   Combination — propagation — affirmation: confused by the different natures of uncertainty

These consequences are most important: the way that combination-propagation-affirmation is done, how the inference procedures, the rules are constructed, how they are based on the uncertainty assignments. In this respect, two basic ambiguities play the major role: the hypothesis of independence of the interacting uncertain events and the exclusion of the middle, i.e. the *closed world assumption*, closed in the sense that events and the dimensions of the event and decision spaces are deemed exhaustive (see further Section 5.12).

The probability archetype model is crisp in both. It can reach conclusions by using logical addition or multiplication, and thus provides data for the interaction of uncertain events with the certainty of the God's-eye view. The probabilistic entailment and Bayesian procedures belong to this class of cases. The D-S* model also uses the combinatorial conclusion model of events, but it deals with the unknown, unexplored regions by smearing probabilities among them using the original guesses about the cases and their supposed coexistence. Other models, such as the game-theoretic and the fuzzy method, calculate minimal and maximal chances, regions of necessity and certainty, as distributions of these chances for consequences instead of clear values.

---

* Here and later the common abbreviation of the Dempster-Shafer method.

Theophrastus and Alexander, disciples of Aristotle, first used a similar notion, expressed later in Latin by *sectetur partem conclusio deteriorem* (the conclusion follows the weaker part), which can be understood as an antecedent of the minimax idea.

As we see the results are not as different as they claim to be. One can be explained by and interchanged with the other's interpretation, with slight changes. As a result, we reach two different attitudes for calculation of consequences after a guess: an evidence estimate, or a statistical probability figure related to the supposed interaction of those events. The first starts with a hypothesis on the nature of the relationships and then calculates a consequence measure by some combination rule which should yield results equal to those of the classical probability calculus in all cases when the conditions are set equally. This is the  Dutch book story: Nobody can win at gambling over a long time against the rules of probability calculus.

The other way can be a reduction of the consequence calculation to the first guess of individual issues: conferring a subjective estimate of consequence not as a result of calculations, but as further statistics, experience, intuition. These values should be checked by further experiments if Destiny permits. (See the old story of the Rabbi and the goose-breeder who asked the Rabbi week after week how to feed geese that were dying one after the other. After the last goose dies, the Rabbi regretfully exclaims: I had so many more ideas!) In a personal talk, *Zadeh* agreed with the logical transfer of subjective fuzzy guesses to the same in consequences. Cognitive psychology proves that this is mostly the human way of reaching conclusions—good or bad.

We should investigate another fuzzy problem of uncertainty—the *different natures* of it and their relations to the methods used. We have hinted several times at the different nature problem. The subject as a whole could also be classified by different aspects, and certainly none of these classifications can be either complete or unambiguously defined. These relationships are mostly connected to the epistemic and ontological nature of uncertainty, i.e. to the uncertainty of knowledge or to the uncertainty of the subject. Nevertheless these relationships are fused as well: If we would know more about the real nature of uncertainty, we would be much more certain! Let us present a seemingly useful classification from our computational point of view:

1.   *Objective*, physical uncertainty as an intrinsic state of elementary particles. The close relationship of this idea to the classical model is the very field of the probability calculus.

2.   Uncertainty due to the theoretical or practical *impossibility of exact calculation* of the state (problems of very high complexity). These are basically not random problems. We have a model of events which is proved (or looks) adequate. The solution can apply randomization (or partial randomization), such as using Monte Carlo methods, but any approximation or model simplification can be helpful. In most cases, a control factor, such as estimation of convergence error, is available as well. This is the case with most complex technological processes and of those new results described in Section 1.2.

3.   Uncertainty due to a level of *complexity* where no reliable model could be established up to now. This is the typical application area of soft methods, guesses, estimates, etc. The

combination of different evidences, different groups of hypothetical reasons, is the background flavor of the D-S methods used so frequently in similar problems. The medical application is typical: MYCIN people emphasize the relation of their Certainty Factor method to the D-S philosophy.

4.   Uncertainty due to other reasons, i.e. the *lack of knowledge*. In this case the problem is unexplored, hidden for the agents, as in e.g. several human procedures where partners of different interest convene, or in research tasks where some relevant details are not clarified. Methods using evidence guesses are preferred here.

5.   Uncertainty due to *subjective* relationships, i.e. human judgements concerning human relations. Most dialogs and reasoning about human responses are typical examples of this kind. The fuzzy methods and endorsement procedures are attractive for these.

This certainly incomplete enumeration and assignment is not even a recommendation, it is useful only to shed some light on an opaque problem, to indicate the uncertainty in the handling of uncertainty by suggesting some essential differences in the nature of uncertainty. In reality we are usually confronted with an uncertain combination of them all.

A slightly different classification of uncertainty sources is given by *Holtzman* [1989] on types of ignorance:

Type of Ignorance	Characteristics	Example(s)
• Combinatorial	Appropriate Model and Solution Method Are Available, but Cannot Compute Answer	Very Large Linear Program
• Watsonian	Appropriate Model Is Available, but Solution Method is Incomplete	Sherlock Holmes and Dr. Watson
• Gordian	Model Is Incomplete	Gordian Knot; Columbus' Egg
• Ptolemaic	Model May Be Complete, but Is Awkward	Ptolemy Versus Copernicus
• Magical	Model Contains One or More Unexplained Elements	Alka-Seltzer
• Dark	Aware of Issue, but No Model Is Available	Life
• Fundamental	Unaware of Issue	— ? —

These differences are the reasons for several paradoxes as well. The *Three Prisoners Paradox* is a good example. One of the prisoners is sentenced, two of them will be freed but they do not yet know the final verdict. One of them receives information that increases his subjective expectation of being sentenced from one in two. The fact that each one has a chance of one in three was not changed by that. The contradiction is hidden by the different natures of uncertainty. In this case type 4 and 5 are confused. Another related issue is that uncertainty is different for different agents, in different contexts, an issue we return to in Chapters 3 and 4. A paradoxical joke of the Hungarian humorist *Karinthy* exemplifies this case: Columbus arrives in America and is welcomed by the aborigines: *Are you really Mr. Columbus? Oh, wonderful, then we are discovered*! So does the saying: Some people's ceilings are other people's floor. In each situation we are confronted with the *different worlds* problem (Section 3.3): We step out of a seemingly closed model and see the same situation from another model's (world's, dimension's) point of view.

After this general discussion, let us review the usually indicated methods but restrict ourselves only to the points of view mentioned above.

2.7 Purist probability — strongest but not almighty

 *Cheeseman* [1985] in a very clear paper argues for the universal validity of the probability concept. The main idea which guarantees an integration of all different approaches is that *probability is the representation of a state of knowledge.** Therefore *the* probability, in a conventional sense, does not exist. Any kind of subjective guess, experience, hypothesis, conclusion based on reasoning, information received from others, hearsay, or statistics can be the source of this knowledge, the state of which is expressed by the probability measure. As this probability can be improved on the same subject, several parallel probabilities can exist as states of knowledge of different people. This kind of probability guess, considered as knowledge acquisition, should be detached from the further action of decision making, which has to weigh the knowledge from different sources, assess

---

* We see that the problem of the agent and context is neglected in the definition.

their risks, etc. In this way, the D-S view of known and unknown, having evidence only for groups of uncertain events, can be resolved in a more cumbersome way if it is really needed; if not, then a much simpler process for having an estimate of the different kinds and groups of uncertainties can be used. The choice of the procedure depends on what effort is practically necessary .

P. Walley [1987] analyzes Dempster's combination rule and criticizes only its major claim, the possibility of combining evidence from independent observations with prior beliefs. It proves to be possible only in cases where the Bayesian procedure is viable and in those cases the results are the same as the Bayesian ones. In this way, one major focus of the unification of all or most different or likely methods is the Bayesian view, treated in a very general way. Slightly modifying Cheeseman's statement: Representation of a state of knowledge is a state of conceptual-experimental-cognitive classification.

As a result of this view, knowledge of distributions can be treated with the usual density functions and, according to the Bayesian philosophy, they can be attached to the decision phase as weights for estimation of sensitivity and reliability of the probability measure.

In evaluation of different probability measures, such as guesses from different sources on the same subject, the methods of *maximum entropy* could be attractive (if it can be done). In this way one chooses those estimates which are calling for the minimal conditional dependence. The entropy concept does not really add relevance to the unification considerations. It can be practical in some computations dealing with logarithms. From a more distant philosophical point of view it is a representation of order and disorder. Order in this sense is related to meaning, structured existence, a possibility of organizing information by rules; disorder means an equal distribution which from another point of view (as we have hinted at in Section 2.4) can be the highest form of Order.

The search for the maximum entropy distribution in a sense conforms to Ockham's Razor principle as well: The maximum entropy distribution carries minimum information among those satisfying the constraints.

Computational difficulties arise in each case of longer logical chains. We meet everywhere, with every theoretically captivating method, the same contradiction: In any practical, realistically complex case we must assign weak estimates to each possible fact, assign or compute estimates for each possible combination of facts, and entail these data among all possible consequences and their combinations. We are quickly lost in a vast forest (metaphorically as well as factually, by graphic representations) of ever weaker estimates, of increasing uncertainty, made opaque by an immense and seemingly convincing computational engine.

This is the reason why we − and many others − have sympathy for greater unification of the methods rather than more diversity, for simpler, short-cut methods, and for a critique from the application point of view rather than looking for increased theoretical elegance.

These interpretations directed toward *unification* can also include the fuzzy set concept. The uncertainty of set membership and the distance between a certain set or element and an ideal prototype (concept) are probabilities in this sense, i.e. representations of the state of knowledge. This trend is especially emphasized in the works of *Dubois* and *Prade*.

The basic convergence is apparent. We look now at the real deviations.

Several excellent papers analyze the pros and cons of different ap-proaches*, comparing cases and interpretations in which they render identical results and those where they diverge. We refer to them here once more for those who would like a more precise picture from the mathematical point of view. Nevertheless we try here to summarize the basic corners of these divergences:

- cases of *low evidence*
- cases of *low confidence* in evidence of any value
- cases of *high complexity* concerning the frames of discernment, high number of possible cases, their common occurrences
- overwhelming contradictory evidence.

Unfortunately, the most practical complex systems embody an almost infinite frame of evidence with many unknown possibilities and ig-norance of mutual dependencies. These all are more or less excluded from the usual calculation models. The exclusion is not because the au-thors ignore these situations but the inadequacy of mathematical meth-ods and a belief that these situations can be approximated by hypoth-eses which are more easily treatable.

All the above four reasons of divergences conclude in one: in-adequate statistics or—formulated in a more precise way—the inherent inadequacy of statistics from the point of view of most decision prob-

---

* [Duda, Hart and Nilsson 1976; Buchanan and Shortliffe 1984; Cheeseman 1985; Goodman and Nguyen 1985; Shafer 1976; Gordon and Shortliffe 1985; Bhatnagar and Kanal 1986; Fung and Chong 1986; Grosof 1986; Kanal and Lemmer 1986; Lemmer 1986; Liu 1986; Wise and Henrion 1986; Zadeh 1986; Shafer 1986; Ihara 1987; Kyburg, Jr. 1987; Shafer and Logan 1987a; Shafer, Lindley and Spiegelhalter 1987b; Walley 1987; Cheeseman, Self, Kelly, Taylor, Freeman and Stutz 1988; Henkind and Harrison 1988; Pearl 1988; Perlis 1988; Smets, Mamdani, Dubois and Prade 1988; Perez 1989]

lems. This is the reason why the enumerated *corners* are the typical weak points of the methods and why these methods offer different results in the neighborhood of these weaknesses. We are not able to produce and process a sufficient amount of information for a reliable prediction, we cannot disclose all possible internal relations, nor provide conditions which are invariant for time and other coordinates. Last but not least, even if we could do all these, then the resulting advice for a decision can only be viable in those cases which permit a statistical error similar to that of the observation itself. The problem is reduced to the Rabbi with endless ideas for feeding the geese.

Statistics is also understood in a broader sense. As we shall see in Chapter 5, the human brain does not work as a simple statistical machine, performing just that kind of weighing and combining of information that leads to our intuitions, beliefs, and evidential feelings. Nevertheless the calculation methods of uncertainty are either based on a statistical model, as the probabilistic approaches are—independent of strict frequency considerations or subjective philosophy—or have no semantic background model at all. Often their semantic models, e.g. scores or polling, are a variant of the statistical one or weaker. This is the case with the Dempster rule of combination as well, as was pointed out by *Shafer* himself. All non-Bayesian methods of combination, i.e. calculation of mutual effects, their inverse, validation, propagation, and affirmation only have the ambition to be consistent from the mathematical/logical point of view. This means, first of all, a method which is monotonic in any case. In other words, the process increases in evidence by additional affirmation; is commutative, independent of the sequence of the information, and associative, not confusing the possibilities of pooling and separating information. A further requirement is a kind of completeness and closed world which includes all available and possible information in a uniform frame. This is expressed by a normalization procedure which provides a unity (usually the value 1) for the global frame in every step of calculation.

These requirements reflect the strength and weakness of all representations. They are mathematically correct, logically feasible, mostly free of contradictions and, by very professional refinements, also free of eventual paradoxes. But none of them can deliver a final answer to the uncertainty of calculation of the consequences of uncertain events or information.

As a consequence, numerical results differ mostly due to the above mentioned problems. A very typical example is the *Certainty Factor* assessment of MYCIN, which cuts off evidence below a 0.2 value. Several investigations studied the relationship of the Dempster's combination rule and the Bayesian calculations. The majority of published results prove that, with some exceptions related to the Zadeh-paradox for marginal values (see Appendix 3) and different estimations for unknown events, they can be transferred into each other. This is done by some extensions of interpretation. Which method should be taken as a standard and which is superior compared to the other depends on the preference of the author. This remark also refers to those publications that pick out cases where differences should be demonstrated.

2.8 Some more epistemic and practical considerations

A major difference between the D-S model and the probabilistic-Bayesian one lies in the diverse interpretation of uncertainty. The probabilistic approach takes chance as *a priori*, given facts about events. Using the popular *Three Prisoners Paradox* mentioned in Section 2.6, all three have an equal chance of being declared guilty or released. This can be modified by later information. According to the D-S model, the prisoners have an incomplete model of possible events and these are combined to get an uncertain possibilistic conclusion. The probabilistic modeler is more like an external observer, the D-S modeler is more internally involved. The first assigns a probability to each branch of his model and calculates the results of their combinations, while the second accepts partial information, information on combinations, and calculates the beliefs in the individual events. The first looks more for the chances, the second more for the provability of supposed events, how the model helps in increasing the belief in one or the other hypothesis. The Bayesian gives an equal chance for cases that are completely unknown, the D-S modeler leaves this completely open for a weighted distribution of further information about these cases. The weighted distribution happens by means of the Dempster-rule of combination, which, though a very plausible one is nevertheless arbitrary. The results of these differences are different conclusions in cases of incomplete information (the case of complete information reduces the D-S model to the Bayesian), sometimes—as *Zadeh* has shown—paradoxical conclusions. Several refinements help to avoid any paradoxical or implausible conclusions of the D-S method. Nevertheless, no final decision can be taken on the validity of these different views.

The clash between the Bayesian and the Dempster-Shafer view becomes apparent—as *Pearl* [1988] points out—in the case of conflicting rules, i.e. at the boarder of monotonicity. The problem of nonmonotonic inference will be the subject of the next chapter, but, as we shall see, the uncertainty of assessment and reasoning are not really separable. The Bayesian view, with its individual guesses, requires a careful but early commitment, while the D-S method offers a normalized but delayed one. The choice depends on the nature of the problem and on the preference of the user.

Another relation of the D-S method also points to the nonmonotonic logic problem. This is the *Truth Maintenance System* (TMS) method (see Appendix 13) as a symbolic engine for computing D-S belief functions. The TMS method of *Doyle* [1979] operates with the combination of coherent evidence. For each logical step, it logs the conditions of validity. In other words, the evidence is clustered as parallel assumptions; if one of the assumptions is followed by a contradiction, the system returns to the next one. In this way the assumptions are checked by their consequences. A further development, the *Assumption-based TMS* (ATMS) [Forbus and de Kleer 1988] carries out this procedure in a more explicit way. The limitations of real alternative approaches is nicely illustrated by this development. The original TMS is a seemingly hard, logic-based system. The resolution of the inherent nonmonotonicity is given by these later works which soften the procedure by numerical assignment; the result is D-S-based techniques. If the procedure is definitely monotonic, the whole game is senseless, since everything can be treated by the simple Bayesian-logical way.

As was mentioned earlier, computational requirements are one of the decision aspects, and this changes as well. For example, algorithms are recommended for avoiding the combinatorial complexity of the D-S method due to the large number of combinations [Shafer and Logan 1987]. The other aspect should be a risk assessment. The same situation can be different for different actors, as was referred to in cases of an internal or external observer. Taking the *Three Prisoners Paradox*, the case is different for the jailer than for the prisoners, different if the prisoner expects capital punishment or a few months sentence. The same can be valid for a medical case, with different conclusions suggested by the physician, the patient, the surgeon, or the internist. In cases where contradictory results are received from different models, first the model should be revised and then risk assessment can help in determining a reasonable choice.

A relevant difference between the usual approaches lies in the handling of *distribution*. This has a clear-cut and mathematically correct treatment in statistics-based probability theory. Applying these methods theoretically we can conclude that as a result of probabilistic events we get a range of possible cases, each with a certain chance, and the accuracy of this calculation has a well-defined confidence. All other approaches hide these different concepts of statistics behind much simpler estimates, weighings, etc. As we tried to point out, this is not rooted in the weakness of the methods but in the nature of uncertainty itself. In any branch of application, a continuous analysis should decide how far we should and can go in the pursuit of hypothetical precision. This depends on the nature of the data and available information, i.e. on the amount, number of relevant types, reliability, constancy, etc.

The same consideration is valid for calculation requirements. Each refinement is burdened by an increased computational need, especially those which try to handle distributions, i.e. spectra of data instead of sharp values and cross-relations, as in the Dempster-Shafer method or any of those which estimate propagation of uncertainty, such as Nilsson's probabilistic logic or Pearl-Kim's propagation schemes. Most of these cases quickly lead to an exponential explosion (computation of all possible cross-relations) and in that way not only to an unsolvable computational task but also to a blurring of the evidence picture. Several algorithms try to find a viable compromise. E.g. the D-S method as it was outlined first involves a combinatorial amount of calculations because it uses the combinations of all beliefs on a hierarchical graph for evidence. This is an obvious consequence of the challenging character of the method: It is supported not only by supposed atomic evidence of singular events but can make inferences based on evidence of event groups. Nevertheless several attempts [Barnett 1981, Gordon and Shortliffe 1985, Shafer and Logan 1987] were made to overcome these difficulties of computation by a rational procedure of problem partitioning, which decreases the exponential to a linear problem. Nevertheless no last word exists in this respect either. A careful analysis of pros and cons in the case concerned cannot be omitted. We must also emphasize that computational requirements are a theoretically decidable problem and this decision can give advice for extreme possibilities or impossibilities. But after that we face a very pragmatic task: What kinds of software are available for our purposes, what are their characteristics, what amount of work is needed in the worst case for expected additional software development, and what is the risk of doing so? All of which can be added to risks of uncertainty in information and theoretical method of handling them.

2.9 Lessons of machine learning

The methods used in machine learning reflect the basic contradictions of all that has been said before. The ingenious model of *L. Valiant* [1987] was duly scrutinized by *Amsterdam* [1988] who concluded that it supposes as biased a model as any other learning procedures, although a different one. The Valiant model is based on statistics of input data (our first source of uncertainty) and declares that: "A learnable concept is nothing more than a short program that distinguishes some natural inputs from some others." What we take as an input (measure, get information, etc.) or how we consider the further evaluation (basic phenomenon, noise, etc.) is not discussed. Input-statistics based learning is reasonable because we can rightly assume that life produces inputs for us using the same distribution during the learning phase as in our adult life (when we are more practitioners than pupils). Here we simply accept the *a priori* as present in the world. Nevertheless all problems of input interpretation — as discussed in this book as well — remain.

The problem is attacked from another side by *R. E. Kalman* [1986] who does not accept the probabilistic models, considering them prejudiced on the relationship between phenomena and noise. Thus, he accepts covariance only. This view takes a quasilinear and stationary model as granted (in tacit knowledge) — no final word, but a circumvention of the same bottomless dark well, with, nevertheless, some more insight in some more cases. We did not mention other earlier and relevant works on learning* because they were not as ambitious as the Valiant claim, they tried to solve some simpler particular problems and had success, to some extent.

2.10   No final conclusion but practical advice—the basic quality of uncertainty is uncertainty itself

What is our final conclusion? What can we give as advice for the user? The very first one is not to be a believer of any one approach, but to be very critical, because there is no final conclusion. **The basic quality of uncertainty is uncertainty itself**. This cannot be circumvented by any highly sophisticated, consistent, logico-mathematically correct method because the model, which is the framework of the method, cannot *per se* be identical with the sublime vaporousness of the real phenomena. If *a priori* and *a posteriori* events were equivalent, then the problem would be solved. But in practice, the experimenter and the decision maker rarely have an equal opportunity to sample and have even less equal risk in the two activities.

This means that no absolute method can be given and most probably can never be. *Henkind* and *Harrison* [1988] conclude the following after a detailed semantic and computational requirement analysis: "There has been an unfortunate tendency to blindly choose an   uncertainty calculus

---

* [Winston 1982; Lenat 1983a-b; Michalski 1983b; Michalski and Dietterich 1985; Michalski, Carbonell and Mitchell 1983; Greiner 1988; Michie 1988]

for incorporation into a knowledge-based system. In particular, some of the commercial expert system shells offer only one calculus (and those with more flexibility give little guidance as to which calculus to choose). We offer the following suggestions.

The *Bayesian calculus* is well-suited for applications where probabilities are known (or can be acquired with a reasonable effort). The calculus is especially attractive because of its strong theoretical foundation (note, however, that the calculus is generally unusable in its purest form due to exponential information complexity).

The *Dempster-Shafer calculus* is a good choice for applications where uncertainty is best thought of as being distributed in sets rather than just single items. Depending upon the particular domain, it can also have acceptable information and time complexity.

The *fuzzy-set calculus* is well-suited for applications where the evidence is itself fuzzy in nature. Fuzzy-set techniques also have the advantages of great flexibility and low information and time complexities.

The main appeal of *MYCIN/EMYCIN model* is its low information and time complexity, and its current wide availability.

Each of the four calculi has a different perspective on uncertainty, and each manipulates uncertain information in a different way. Despite what some authors have claimed there does not seem to be one calculus that is 'the best' for all situations. Each of the calculi has its strong points; the main disadvantage that we see in all of the calculi is that they compute aggregate numbers but keep no record of divergence in opinions."

Other methods are not discussed here because of the lack of experience. This experience is specially important because of the nature (and natures) of uncertainty. A method can be theoretically firm, the model clear and attractive, but only experience can reveal all hidden problems.

Some further recipes can be offered, based on the above partly subjective considerations and these should be also taken with salt and pepper:

1. As far as it is possible (there exists a relatively reliable statistics of *a priori* and the computational efforts are not excessive compared to the values in question) use *Bayesian methods*. This is the only one which has a very firm logico-mathematical background, a vast literature of sensitivity, special cases, and, what is most important, it has a semantics. It can be matched to a *prima facie* understandable model, i.e. the comparison with any previous and further knowledge on the system is easy.

2. If there is much more uncertainty in the data, we have mere estimates, beliefs rather than real statistics, and if the region (possible cases) of uncertainty can be somehow described, the Dempster-Shafer approach may be advisable. The D-S method is specially appropriate if we have an estimate on groups of events but not on individual ones. This method is closest to the Bayesian, well-established, widely used, and analyzed. Special attention should be given to components of extreme values (e.g. low evidence) and to computational complexity.

3. If *uncertainty* is still *higher* (what an uncertain statement!), with practically no statistics available except estimates, beliefs based on practical experience, and the sensitivity of these estimate combinations is not too high, a *MYCIN-like CF method can be used*; it is well biased towards marginal values, its computational requirement is matched to the expected reliability of computational results, the model of events is well preserved transparently during the whole procedure, i.e. it can be checked for feasibility and corrected at every phase of calcula-

tion and especially at the resulting recommendations. This can be taken as a brute force method.

4. As was discussed before, the *fuzzy* concept is different more in philosophy than in calculation methods. The latter are approaching the classical mathematical procedures of Bayesian statistics, game theory, and Dempster-Shafer methods. The philosophy is, nevertheless, very important. We tried to show that this semantics is crucial in the building and evaluation of the event model.

5. If someone does not have a brilliant new idea or does not encounter a practical case which is completely different from any previous models, they should be *warned against* any attempt *to develop further methods*. We have seen the basic, final unsolvability of the uncertainty problem and the specific pitfalls due to this essential, intrinsic issue. It can, therefore, be extremely dangerous to abandon the abundant experience of well-elaborated, widely used methods which have avoided or at least measured these pitfalls. A new method can be a red herring, a vain pursuit of a quasi-optimal model of the events.

Thus we can only draw attention to the importance of checking our models, by further data, by other investigations, and by common sense. Most important is that in the region of uncertainty, nothing can be considered more than a hypothesis. Because we meet uncertainty nearly everywhere, this statement is generally valid for all our knowledge, and especially so for those areas which are results of computation.

> "It used to be said, that God could create everything, except what was contrary to the laws of logic. The true is we could not say of an 'unlogical' world how it would look."
>
> *Wittgenstein: Tractatus logico-philosophicus, 3.031*

Chapter 3
Logic and its relativity*

3.1 The horror and the pitfall of uncertainty

 Expert systems are primarily based on logic. This is due to several historical reasons. One of them is the long lasting belief of European intellectuals in the supremacy of logic over any other kind of reasoning. The other reason, outlined by *Shafer* [1987b], can be described in a crude way as a horror of uncertainty. As we shall see in Chapter 5, this does not lack a reason. Logic later started to be combined with one or anoth-

---

* Similar to Chapter 2 a short review is given of the major subjects in the Appendix for those who are not familiar with one or the other method. This is done in the following sequence:

lambda calculus	Appendix 7
nonmonotonic logic	Appendix 8
circumscription	Appendix 9
default logic	Appendix 10
autoepistemic logic	Appendix 11
counterfactuals	Appendix 12
Truth Maintenance Systems	Appendix 13
paradoxes	Appendix 14

er interpretations of uncertainty, and that is the topic of this chapter. This was the swamp where people lost the certainty lent them by the belief in the supremacy of logic. The latest reason for sticking to logic was the basically logical nature of the digital computer.

Both the superficial common belief in the ubiquity of logic and its superior power, and the doubts surrounding pure logical inference have a long history. They accompanied the whole evolution of logic, from the very start of human thinking. It is not surprising that this ambivalent attitude has returned once more thanks to the fast career of expert systems development. Nevertheless, it is intriguing that everything had to be reinvented. Very few people gave warning of problems which were well-known much earlier. The euphoria, the publicity boom, and a striving for individual prestige hid nearly all the background from the broader, uninformed public.

We do not intend to give a comprehensive historical review of the development of logic, which has already been done by several authors, notably *W.* and *M. Kneale*'s seminal work [1971]. Our hints should only draw attention to this recurrence of ideas and to the deep well of human thinking worth drawing from. This well also serves as a critical mirror, and stimulates a modest amount of self-criticism.

Most expert systems apply the simple IF ... THEN constructs that are the programmed version of the first, Aristotelean syllogistic scheme (later called the *modus ponens* or by the acronym *Barbara*). Proof or disproof was based on the resolution principle, looking for the existence of false conclusions by converting the initial statements to their negation. (If it is *not* raining, one can *not* be wet).

The hard logic approach of proving by refutation returns us to the origins of logic, the Aristotelean scheme of the *modus tollens* and to the ancient idea of *reductio ad absurdum*, or *reductio ad impossible*, first

referred to by *Zeno of Elea* (c.490-c.430 BC). The supposed first philosophical meaning of dialectics covered the same methodical concept.

Philosophers and historians of philosophy from this early period
discuss different interpretations of the Greek classics. Each would like
to attribute to the original, partly preserved, partly translated later texts
an interpretation similar to that of his age, or just the contrary. This
depends on the intention of the interpreter, whether he would prefer to
get an endorsement from the past or to demonstrate his own new contribution. Unfortunately we cannot consult Aristotle, or the Stoics,
about what they were thinking. Even the specialized meanings of single
words are sometimes dubious, and interpretations within the *Organon*
look different as well e.g. in the *Topica* or the *First* and the *Posterior
Analytics*. Nevertheless, these deviations, and especially the discussion
related to *Plato, Aristotle*, the *Stoics*, and other schools, indicate clearly
that the basic methods and the essential problems concerning them
were more or less clear at this time. According to a witty remark of *F.
Bródy*, if *Aristotle* rose again and got reacquainted with achievements of
science during the past 2300 years, he could understand what we are
thinking of.

We do not want to get any more deeply involved in these further
unresolvable discussions of interpretation. From our point of view, the
emphasis on ancient roots and continuity has a practical meaning for a
computerized future, a warning calling for more modesty (a recurrent
notion in this book), and signals a need to recognize and preserve attitudes of organic development and cultural continuity.

3.2 Relativity and subjectivity

What is wrong here? We discussed earlier the case of the uncertainty of statements, i.e. that we cannot predict if it will be raining in five minutes with an absolute certainty, nor can we recollect with total sureness facts about rain at any earlier time or other place. Uncertain propositions cut or more smoothly divide reasoning into branches of possible events, prescribing a sequence following the uncertainty measures—first, reasoning based on the assumption of rain, because it has a high probability (evidence, belief, etc.), then the less certain case of no rain. Even in this case we can encounter difficulties due to the characteristics of the rain: Is it a heavy shower, a drizzle, hail, etc.?

The basic trouble starts with truth values. Logic is essentially binary, supposing something to be either true or false, and the hypothesis of the excluded middle is a dogma supporting the whole edifice. It can be argued that we moderns have developed many-valued logic as well [Rescher 1969], but there is an essential deviation between those many-valued logics which can be resolved to an *n-1* sequence of binary statements, and those where this reduction cannot be correct. In reality, true and false can be distinguished in a clear-cut way only in very simple and final cases. The exact demarcations are revisited time after time in these cases as well. Let us think about legal-ethical discussions on the beginning and end of life as an example. In most cases it is blurred by uncertainty which relates to measurement and sensing. But, as we have discussed at length in this essay, this easily conceived first uncertainty is really the first cover of *truth* or *falsity*.

A relativity among *syllogisms* (logic programming structures in our computer world) was established by the *modalities*, i.e. those forms which state what kind of conclusion is the result of applying the logical pattern or scheme. In Aristotelean logic, there are some forms of reasoning which yield *necessary* results, some only *possible* ones, others, even weaker, merely do *not exclude* a consequence. These basic modalities were widely extended by the Stoics and logicians of the Middle Ages. A different modality is used in legal reasoning, where the proposition is either *forbidden* or *permitted* but can also be *tolerated* or *motivated*. Evolution of logic provided several other modalities, different ways of using simple syllogistic schemes depending on the contextual framework or application of the usage. All these developments are formulated and treated in detail in any textbook of logic.* We only refer to them here without copying what is common to all curricula of courses in logic. Our main aim is to cast some light on uncertainty which is *not* closely related to the measurement or estimation issue, i.e. to the question of how reliable the data are, but that have a contextual dependency. This is the case described as the second reflection in Section 1.1. It is a different phenomenon from other kinds of reflection-mapping problems.

As we now know, objective and subjective cannot be clearly segregated, because we cannot handle anything which is not reflected in our mind. This duality has a parallel in modal and intensional logic. Modal logic is more closely related to objective usage conditions, while intensional logic lies closer to the subjective ones. Basically they are the

---

* [Church 1941; Quine 1950; Tarski 1956; Kleene 1967; Barwise 1974; Ruzsa 1981; Thayse 1988]

same: a conditional mode of application of the logical schemata. Most important is the acknowledgement of this conditional reality, the eclipse of the belief in the transcendental existence of logic as a law of the universe. For us, this means as a consequence a critical view of all logic-based computational results. *Goethe*'s version: "The phenomenon does not segregate itself from the observer, on the contrary, it will be interwoven and complicated with his personality." (*Maxims and Reflections*).

This subjectively flavored intensional logic has several interpretations which appear under different nomenclatures, notations, and, typically, as discoveries of different people, but it carries essentially the same content: a relativity of reasoning due to human circumstances.

Let us investigate three conceptual frameworks of the same sort: the Kripke-logic [1972] of possible worlds, the Montague-logic [1974] of possible interpretations, and the Barwise-Perry logic [1983] of possible situations. These ideas are not new, even in Artificial Intelligence literature. They were detailed in *McCarthy* and *Hayes'* paper, quoted several times here. (There are many other ramifications, such as the discourse-logic, etc., but from our point of view, the opposite process, the reduction to the trunk and the roots, is important. Something in a ramification could be important if it can lead us to the root of a really different trunk.)

These ideas also have long antecedents. The fundamental issue is the fact that the meanings of words, sentences, and texts change with time, cultural and emotional conditions, different sources of knowledge, from person to person, and from community to community. The consequence of this fact is that a true logical proposition in one relationship can be false in another.

3.3 The result: different worlds

Kripke defines different possible worlds. The idea can be twisted in many amusing ways, as *Kripke* did in his famous story about a French boy who read about a dazzling city called Londres. By chance, he was brought to London, to a shabby suburb where he had a hard life, forever sighing for the splendid "Londres" of his dreams. As we see, the same concept (the city) has two names, but the same name can cover two opposite realities.

The idea of different possible worlds is an old one as well. We trace it back to *Giordano Bruno*, but certainly he had several antecedent sources as well. *Leibniz* used this idea in a different way. His purpose was the surmounting of uncertainty. He argued that God had not created an uncertain world, but He could have produced an infinite number of worlds. We are living in the best possible of them. This statement is not the same one *Voltaire* mocked in *Candide*; it contained profound thoughts about maximal and minimal possibilities, about teleology and final constraints—all our own problems, of course, in a conceptually pre-modern formulation. An ingenious French author, *Bernard le Bovier de Fontenelle* (1637-1757), wrote a scientific popularization: *Entretiens Sur Le Pluralité Des Mondes* (Conversations about the Multitude of Worlds) and, in another book, *Dialogues Des Morts* (Dialogues of the

Dead) coined the witty sentence: "As far as roses remember, no gardener ever died."

The idea of realistic different worlds is recurrent. We use them in the conceptual sphere but some interpretations of quantum mechanics refer to a simultaneous possibility of different states. *Hofstadter* [1981] quotes Hugh Everett's proposal of 1957 in the book edited by Bryce S. Dewitt and Neill Graham titled: The Many-Worlds Interpretation of Quantum Mechanics.

Much can be argued (and has been) on the real existence of different worlds, their relations to possible worlds, and the subjectivity of the concept, but from our point of view this is immaterial—the only important issue is the relativity in and of our programs in different environments.

Montague draws attention to the different names for the same object, returning to the old paradigm of *Phosphorus* and *Hesperus*. The names of the *Morning* and *Evening Star* were, for a long time, not known to be the same astronomical object. We can add that it is not even a star but a planet, Venus.

The *situational logic* of *Barwise* and *Perry* [1983] emphasizes the fact that any kind of statement and reasoning is dependent on the situation. If somebody on the earth lets a glass slip, the situation is very different from what happens onboard a space ship.

All these look very trivial and the interpretation above of deep logical and technical considerations is intentionally trivial. This interpretation would like to show that the problems are obvious, but it covers the difficulties of coping with them.

The techniques have two difficulties, the first is minor compared to the other more major one. This minor problem lies in the application of embedded logical expression. For example, IF object (IF object is glass

(IF object is on board of a spaceship)) is let slip THEN it most probably will *not* be broken. In a case where all conditions can be evaluated independently, the expression can be resolved into a sequence of first-order logic and the problem is reduced to regular schemes of, e.g., *Horn-clauses** used in PROLOG. If this cannot be done (the conditions are somehow looped), higher order logic should be applied with all its difficulties of implementation. We shall see that in nonmonotonic logic where the outcomes may be contradictory, we find such looped situations. The real world is more nonmonotonic than straightforward.

3.4 The binding problem

We have reached the binding problem. In general we are speaking about objects, which are, e.g. slipping. When we bind the concept *object* to glass, we are thinking in general of actions on the earth's surface, but now we bind the action to a place with different gravitational conditions. If this binding can be done immediately, we do not care about these problems. In common sense action, the human mind executes all these bindings in parallel and does the feasibility check as well by handling a familiar scenario. In Chapter 4 we return to this human way of problem solving and speak more about why the hu-

---

* *Horn-clause*: A clause is a disjunction of a finite number of literals or propositions notated by these literals. A Horn-clause is a clause having at most one positive literal, i.e. it is a simple rewriting rule for logical inference and by that virtue used in the logic programming language PROLOG (e.g. get wet *if* raining, no umbrella, no arcade).

man mind works mostly *in concreto*, without these cumbersome logical procedures. A computer in the same situation will be either dull or mad if it could not be programmed in an appropriate way. For a very limited flexibility of adaptation, it needs a high complexity of operations.

A fixed binding needs an exact, unambiguous definition of the predicates and exact, unambiguous data for these definitions. E.g.: A glass can be either very fragile or practically unbreakable because the concept *glass* can cover different compositions of materials. For a more complex system, the binding should be left open until the last possible moment (analogous to the dynamic programming principle) to remain flexible enough. Some of the definitions and data acquisition can be recursive and because of that we miss the possibility of the application of simple logical expressions (see Appendix 7). The technology of binding is solved by the *lambda* calculus or by any kind of variation of the same. A vast mathematical literature on the *lambda* calculus and the related recursive functions mark those problems at which we have only hinted.*

The minor problem leads to the major one. Each world, each distinction of meaning, each situation requires separate definitions of the concepts, separate sets of data, and a vast amount of semaphores, switches, demons. All these very quickly introduce a combinatorial explosion. No generally usable practical remedy exists. We come back to the basic problem of this book and of epistemology: Either we try to put all foreseeable different cases with all possible consequences into computer memory, or we try to find a General Divine Rule (or a few of

---

* [Kleene 1936; Church 1941b; Péter 1967; Frege 1879; Rosser 1984; Barendregt 1984]

them) which could derive all these possibilities by calculation based on some actual data. *John von Neumann* made a remark in the very early days of computers and of thinking about relationships between Nature and computers: It can be supposed that the minimal realization of the visual perception is the visual cortex. We could extend this not yet refuted hypothesis that the computational complexity of the Universe may not be dramatically less than the Universe itself. Anyone can argue that we have arrived at a philosophical concept of God. Nothing can be stated to the opposite.

As mentioned before, from our point of view nonmonotonic logic is an issue related to the general problem of the relativity of logic. Each special logical form has a paradigmatic example such as the *mortality of Socrates*, or *Achilles and the turtle*. Here we meet the case of Tweety*, a favorite penguin-like figure of American children. The penguin is a bird which cannot fly, although birds generally fly. We can also interpret the problem in the terms used previously: The meaning of the word *'fly'* is different for people who only observe behavior and for those who get into biological details. Take a different aspect: For all people on the European continent (this was *the* world for a long time for Europeans) all birds fly, while an antarctic world contains flying and non-flying birds, in some regions there may be more non-flying birds than flying ones. The case is similar for a situation as for a world: walking in a continental forest, or living in the Galapagos Islands. Several methods have been developed for overcoming this common difficulty, such as *the default*

---

* What a nice example for these considerations and later of Section 4.8! My American editor, *A. B. Brodsky* comments here: the cartoon Tweety is a flying parakeet; Opus is a comic strip penguin (Bloom County) — and he is right, thanks — but the current literature uses Tweety everywhere for this paradoxical metaphor!

logic of *Reiter* [1980] or *circumscription* by *McCarthy* [1980]. As we mentioned in Section 2.8, *Truth Maintenance Systems* are related both to monotonic and nonmonotonic problems. All basically apply the above methods. The default is a special switch construct for exceptions or for a neutral noncontradictory case, TMS and circumscription use logical and storage apparatus to search for a noncontradicting case, a solution, or a proof.

The different world concept can and should be extended for reasoning considering time, as *McDermott* [1982], *Y. Shoham* [1988] and several others before him did as quoted in the seminal paper of *McCarthy* and *Hayes*. The *Yale Shooting Problem* described in Appendix 14 was coined to illustrate the problem which, although similarly not original with him, was most concisely described by the statements of *Heraclitus* (c.535-c.475 B.C.) that "Everything flows and nothing stays." (Plato, Cratylus, 402a) or "You cannot step twice into the same river." Not surprisingly, the implementation methods are rather similar to all nonmonotonic logic and related problems. Nevertheless we can return here to the Stoics as well as we do by the *Horned paradox* in the next section. By some substitutions you find it to be the same as the Yale Shooting Problem, nevertheless more than two millennia earlier and as *Plato* refers to even further in the deep well of human thought.

We are deliberately not going into technical details since these can be found in the literature cited. Our main concern is not to provide a textbook on the topic or a disciplined extension of existing instruments, not even a general epistemology, but rather a bird's eye view on those aspects which are hidden, precisely as a result of the problems of practical computer usage and are not sufficiently treated due to this gap between practical computer science, mathematics and philosophy.

In this essay we try to put the different branchings of the relativity of logic into a more or less unified framework. This may help the readers and the users of the methods to not get lost in the abundance of the glamorous namings of similar ideas. The objective was the same as in Chapter 2 with the different uncertainty methods. The historical perspective helps to do the same as was done by the methodological perspective, therefore we risk only a slightly ironic remark: All people inventing various kinds of nonmonotonic logic should also remember the philosophers of the Middle Ages, from *Abelard* through *William of Shyreswood* to *Ockham*, struggling against very similar difficulties.

3.5 Paradoxes: the mirrors of Logic's relativity

A relevant topic of logic is related to paradoxes. The contributions of paradoxes have been of paramount importance to the development of logic. The quest for their resolution has inspired much of what we possess at present as tools, concepts of logic. With the advent of Artificial Intelligence they have acquired important practical aspects as well. We shall turn now to the renewed forms of those paradoxes discovered mostly by the Sophists of Greece. In this chapter, however, we emphasize only the traps and deficiencies, as caveats to the unconditional belief in logical inference. Paradoxes, contradictory results of seemingly correct entailments, arise from several different reasons and are treated in various ways.

Any uncertainty can lead to paradoxes. The nature of these uncertainties was the subject of the previous chapter. Therefore no reasoning based on uncertain roots can be treated as certain, nor can reasoning based on accepted, seemingly certain roots be considered free from possible uncertainties — one reason why we should treat every result as a more or less reliable hypothesis. The uncertainty is a kind of a demon opening and closing doors to different worlds. We never know which world we are entering, the paradox is a situation of stepping into an unexpected world.

The different world, meaning or situation case — if hypothetically consistent — provides contradictions as it meets another world, meaning or situation, if two closed worlds have any communication or overlapping. This is obvious. All kinds of human conflicts and negotiations are rich examples. Truth, in general, is a questionable human concept concerning the ever changing, continuously moving, infinite aspects of reality and the limits of human cognition, but truth in human affairs is *per se* a relativistic idea, valid only from the point of view of one person, one group, one certain time, one certain situation. One can argue that this may be valid in humanistics, but what does it have to do with engineering, for example? No engineering task is free from those human aspects: Prices and other components of economics work by very subjective human feedback, the interests of manufacturers, the environment, or users are all individual, time (e.g. seasonally) and culturally dependent contradictory items.

Decision support systems*, which mostly combine game theoretical and knowledge-based methods, provide a broad spectrum for problem solving in multi-objective optimization tasks. The game models are beautiful, but poor for the treatment of realistic manifolds; they apply mostly to linear or quasilinear approximations and meet with a multi-

---

* [Neumann and Morgenstern 1947; Bonczek, Holsapple and Whinston 1981; Hipel and Fraser 1984; Sage 1987]

tude of the difficulties discussed in the chapter on uncertainty. All are loaded with the logical ambiguities of the knowledge bases: principles, different habits of reasoning, interests, etc. This is not an argument against the use of decision support systems—just the contrary! If they are used in the right way, they should discover hidden contradictions, explain the reasons for different outcomes, and help to make the subjective feeling somehow more objective. They would then fill a glorious role. Most important is the conscious insight into the nature of contradictions!

Let us look at a typical technical task, where the coherent existence of different worlds was supposed—robot control. The hypothesis would be that a world (a problem area, a certain scenario of unilateral action, a sequence of events with no human interaction) can be created where everything is well-defined, the conceptual relationships of the definitions do not change during the observation of the world, and the world is closed, i.e. no definition is required for action from outside if the initial state and the laws, the rules of possible actions, are set. An excellent demonstration was the block world of robot action created by *T. Winograd*. All possible objects (cube, pyramid, etc.), their relevant attributes from the point of view of command communication (color, size) and with regard to motion (surfaces) could be defined, as could types of actions (lift), laws related to possible situations of the objects (e.g. which one can and cannot support or contain the other). Unfortunately, this was probably the ultimate complexity of a task which could be treated in that way. *Winograd* who was interested more in natural language understanding than robotics, investigated the references of pronouns using this very low-complexity experiment, a simple case of the more general reference problem. Even in this particular case, he has shown that a different context for the same sentences can mean something terribly different. This was at the time of *Nasser* and *Khrushchev*, and the sentence: "The red block supports the pyramid", had a political meaning as well. How time dependent, even in so short a historical period!

A favorite metaphor of Operations Research is similar: The problem of the *Byzantine Generals*. Several generals are cooperating, but one (or a few) of them can be a traitor (or unreliable). What should be the optimal strategy be for avoiding the consequences of this uncertain condition? [Lamport, Shostak and Pease 1982] Any device, especially any control equipment of a coordinated system, can behave itself as a Byzantine general.

The more closely we look at the overall robot control problem, the more we see that it is not yet solved in any general way (by some general algorithm, or knowledge) in spite of the tremendous efforts made by control people. The problems are even further complicated if two hands must be coordinated. The two-handed coordination (especially if they are separate) needs to get continuous information on the other hand's situation, on the world as it is recognized (e.g. by its own dedicated sensors), and on the intentions of the other operator. The scenario is more complicated if the movement of the object(s) due to external forces (e.g. gravitation, impulses exerted by one of the robot hands) or internal ones (elasticity, motors, etc.) were to be considered (a third world).

This problem has a previous paradigm as well; the story of the *Allied Generals*: Two are allies against one, but the two are separated, on different sides of their opponent. They need some time to send messages about their intentions. They can only win if the attack is perfectly coordinated. *Halpern* and *Moses* [1984] have shown that a perfect, absolutely sure coordination is impossible if there is any time delay in communication.

We can add that the results are equally valid due to the impossibility of perfection in describing the situation. This apparently simple, deterministic problem of unmanned robot control is very instructive. We face a problem where the physical laws, i.e. mechanics, kinematics, are quite well known and relatively easy to compute; all phenomena are linear across a wide range. Think about complex chemical, or physical processes, where nonlinearities, chaotic behavior, etc. are not only present but decisive!

The closed world assumption, a firm knowledge of all possible finite events, which governs all logic, is an extension of the excluded middle dogma. They are typical simplifications for model building.

It is now obvious that the idea of different possible worlds is not simply a matter of subjective imagination but is also far from being a deficiency of human intellectual and psychological nature. It is deeply connected with all kinds of reality matching, modeling, and intersystem communication based on these matching transformations. Uncertainties within sensory systems are different, not only due to technological differences or physical phenomena but also because there are different models of the world. Any sensory system, natural or artificial, is developed, designed for a certain purpose or for adaptation to a certain environment. The human visual system is an excellent example. The differences in spectrum sensitivity, view angle, focusing, etc., between the human system and that of other creatures is the first stage of this specialization. The visual cortex, in its highly complex processing capabilities, reflects those experiences which are phylogenetically and ontogenetically collected in our adaptation compulsions. All phenomena of the psychology of vision, such as illusions, are related to these predetermined models, modified by experience, but subjectively biased. The perception of each person is somehow different in this way.*

The same is true for any technological sensory system. The relationships are, of course, much less complex. Instrumentation in a plant or factory is designed for a model of control. Several parameters are measured in an indirect way because there is no practical means for a direct measurement, hence these transformations are hypothesis-model-based as well. As a most simple example, let us quote the case of the above mentioned two-hand robot system equipped with two cameras. The location and mobility of the cameras are based on the task model, the visual conception of the two camera pictures is a terribly simplistic analogy of the human visual perception, but, as anybody who has had to implement the task can say, from the computational point of view it is extremely complex and ambiguous.

To understand the troubles with different worlds we have to go back to the mono-world. The calamity here is a twofold one related to the borders of the world, the previously mentioned problem of closure. If a world can be really closed, then it must have borders. Do they belong to the world inside or to the world outside? The problem was formulated exactly in mathematics as a paradox of set theory: Is the set of all sets given by a certain definition covered by the definition itself or not? Does the set of all sets exist or not? The famous *Russell-paradox* is a nice example: A barber in a village declares that he is shaving all and only those people who do not shave themselves. But what about the barber himself? These open questions led to *Gödel's theorem* [1931], which

---

* [Tversky, Slovic and Kahneman 1982; Gregory 1967, 1977; Crick, Marr and Poggio 1980; Marr 1982; Arbib and Hanson 1988]

may be considered one of the most important innovations in epistemology since the Greeks. No really closed world exists. Any system of axioms can generate a theorem which cannot be proven within the framework of the the referenced axiomatic world. More precisely: In a (sufficiently rich) theory—theory being understood in the precise mathematical sense (see the remark at the end of Section 1.1)—one can always formulate a theorem, whose truth or validity cannot be proven in the system. We quoted some examples from physics in Section 2.1, e.g. numbers (relations) which can be physically generated but are not computable by an algorithm. Tasks which are not solvable within the framework of the task were found by *Church* [1936] and others. The *halting problem* [Turing 1936] is a nice illustration: It was proved that there does not exist any *general* programs (no individual programs are concerned) which can decide if another program will ever halt or not for any legal input of the program.

These are most beautiful but rather difficult mathematical considerations and proofs. For our purposes it is sufficient to be aware of their existence and of the consequences: Even in the mono-world there exist several problems which are theoretically undecidable. On the other hand for most practical problems we find an at least approximative solution but the particular nature of these solutions introduces new constraints, new hypothetical conditions which can be valid in a certain world (environment, model) but not in another.

The Russell-paradox is in some sense a reformulation of one of the oldest: the *Cretan Liar*, and it gained a new timeliness in computer systems as the problem of self-reference. In a closed system, as in a society where everybody is a consistent liar, the relations of truth

and falsity are unambiguous, equivalent to a society of consistently vera-
cious people. In some Turkish cultures, for example, the ways of nod-
ding for yes or no are opposite to the European habit, and their communication is unambiguous, if they do not meet people of other cultures.
Problems start if the two systems meet along a border that implies a
self-reference (as with Russell's barber, who is part of the system himself, there could be a group of such barbers). We see how the different
worlds' idea is related to the self-reference problem: Different worlds
can have different references and a conflict starts at any intersection of
the two worlds. This has been the reason for most of mankind's conflicts
and is now a renewed phenomenon in every system of independent (or
independently designed) components. The Liar's paradox, the Russell-
paradox, and the paradoxes of different worlds appear in our computerized systems as interface problems with interfacing programs, program components, and interconnections with physical systems.

We can find also an uncertainty variant of the Liar's paradox
among the four types of *Eubulides* paradoxes. This is the *Hooded* story:
"You state that you know your brother. But the man who came around and his face
was covered, was your brother and you did not recognize him" (*Lucianus: Bión
Praxis*, 22). Translated to our problems, this story means an uncertain
reference taken as certain because it was received from a generally reliable source. This situation is rapidly spreading; the amount of knowledge which should be used in every single task is unmanageable, and
sources cannot be checked. Knowledge-based systems start to provide
these as a real-time service (e.g. an EKG, or EEG analysis) — the basis
of the knowledge base is hooded! The original metaphor was used for
incomplete reference description but, as we discussed earlier, such an
interpretation does not differ from our views on uncertainty.

A slightly different paradox of *Eubulides,* the *Horned,* is related to the reference problem as well: "What you have not lost, you have it. But you have not lost horns, i.e. you still have horns." (*Diogenes Laertius, lib. VII. 187*) These kinds of references are problems for temporal logic and the closed world assumption. At each instance we meet such surprises, which are trivial for a pragmatic human actor equipped with broad, tacit knowledge, but are paradoxes, sources of deadlocks, and contradictions for artificial systems that rely only on programmed information. By a further generalization we return to the different worlds idea. A programmed machine world meets a real one, equipped with all kinds of facts (knowledge) that were not considered for the machine world. As we shall discuss later, in Chapter 5, a brilliant newborn (such as the computer) must compete with the result of a hundred million years of adaptation and learning.

A further sophistication of the self-reference problem is belief reflexivity, discussed especially by people working in situation and dialog logic. This means that an actor has a belief about the belief of another and vice versa. Further, this is a multiple mirage-mirror phenomenon of different worlds' meetings. The recommended methods of description and orientation are basically not different from all others using lambda-calculus, higher order logic and uncertainty estimates.

3.6 Another aspect of the same issue: nonmonotonic logic

Nonmonotonic logic is an issue often circumvented by modern logicians and artificial intelligence research in particular. The reason is the same group of phenomena we have met before: This problem involves uncertainty and the contradictions of the intrinsically dualistic-causal logic of thinking, i.e. the contradictions between a transcendental divine-human order and that of the real world. Because of its importance we return to the problem of Section 3.2 from another aspect.

Two approaches exist. The first allows no compromise. If a logical structure contains a contradictory, incorrect element, the original assumption is refuted, and a new conceptual model without contradiction must be constructed. This means the original concept must be purified, inheritance definitions restricted to that extent that all consequences remain coherent. This rigor would be ridiculous in the case of our prototype: *Tweety*, the penguin. Either we should exclude the penguin from the class of birds or flying should not be a characteristic attribute. Nevertheless, in programming we tend to follow this puristic way. There are several other technical examples in which a sharp conceptual restriction is much more practical than a flexible general usage.

The second approach is more compliant. It permits *exceptions* in the form of defaults, circumscription and other methods. In the logical, graph-oriented way of thinking, this means a possible deviation in the graph of reasoning. This is much the way common sense works prior to any computer logic. First take the usual path, the obvious or habitual, and then see whether it works or not. If it does not work, discover why, under what conditions it happens, and then choose other paths, one after another, in a sequence that compromises higher chances of success with lower risk.

The only problem with this obvious and practical procedure is the same as in its everyday usage: An exception in a certain environment can be the major case in another context. The duckling follows the first moving body it sees after birth, and recognizes it as a mother during its whole life, but will do the same for any surrogate. The problem is solved, seemingly, by *Pearl*, who includes the exceptions as lower probability branches into the probabilistic reasoning graphoid. The difference in procedures lies not only in their philosophy—in a similar fashion, societies can look at certain attitudes as either another way of life or as a deviation—but also in control of the search for à solution on the graph model. This means control of the practical management of the number of search steps, preserving the clarity of the scheme by avoiding unforeseen loops and the nuisance of backtracking.

All this looks very clear at first sight. Nevertheless, we have to think about why excellent people in nonmonotonic logic seem to avoid this problem, why they so definitely refuse any probabilistic interpretations. The major reason—we suppose—is not a selfish attitude of claiming originality, but the previously mentioned psychological abhorrence of uncertainty. This is based on those facts about uncertainty which were discussed in Chapter 2: the asymmetry of chance and behavior between periods of information collecting and action. The former can be a precise statistical sampling, a logico-mathematical reasoning based on a well-grounded theoretical hypothesis, a personal impression, information collected from textbooks, other resources, or a kind of instinct deeply rooted in our cultural, precultural, or animal past. Examples might include a forecast for population policy, calculation of the trajectory of a ballistic missile, experience with bus frequency at a certain station, practice with spot removal, or caution about some smells. All this information, more or less uncertain due to the uncertainty of the resources, the perception, the circumstances, etc., receives a definite role in a later period of action. The observation view of the certainty of information must be different from the consequence view of risk assessment in applying it.

This consideration is somehow reflected in the *Ace of Spades* paradox. Any card in a deck of 52 has a probability of 1/52 from the observation perspective; from the consequence perspective, the probability of the ace's appearance is either 0 or 1.

The horror of probability and the Janus-face of uncertainty is also based on the probabilistic handling of subclasses in the general problem of inheritance. The exceptions, precisely those subclasses that are confusing clear, logical procedures, differ from the basic convention mostly by their dissimilar properties regarding expected consequences. A bird that flies can easily avoid an approaching car—can survive with a high probability. A bird that does not fly has a low probability of survival.

All these issues would seem void, a mere meditation on trivial facts, except for the fact that a reasoning machine could be very dangerous if it, or its user, is not prepared for them. Any malady is an exception to a healthy state, and has different rules as a result. Atypical forms of an illness require different treatments and may have consequences different from typical ones. It is these atypical consequences that cause the most trouble in medicine. The diagnostic and emergency control procedures for any complex machine have similar features. The most dangerous malfunctions are the low probability ones, and they are most often associated with an avalanche of other complications that are rarely or never expected. In several low probability cases the risks are high, and, as we have seen in Chapter 2, it is just these marginal value cases that are the least computable. The confidence of estimates concerning combination and propagation is very low. We can speak here not only about a non-monotonic case but also about an unstable one. Any logic wobbles in such situations.

3.7 Nonmonotonic logic or probabilistic reasoning

The orthodox nonmonotonic logic approach tries to resolve the problem by saying that the regular case (e.g. that birds fly) is a convention, used for the efficiency of information. All other cases are classified (and defined) as exceptions. This kind of presentation could be easily demonstrated by an airline or train schedule. Nevertheless we have to add to this complete — and completable — data base the different conventions caused by irregularities: Such as those which change the regular convention (e.g. no flights on a few national holidays). These can have inconvenient consequences if not mentioned or add some convenience on certain occasions. The printer of the timetable must take care to preserve the relevant differences.

If a complete data base is available, the timetable can follow a simple procedure: List all regular flights and ask people to inquire at the booking office for schedules on each national holiday — an exception, conditional extension, default statement. The method works if all conditions for exceptions are clearly defined and supposed to be certain. Can the reader imagine a schedule with remarks for fog, congestion, snow, etc? How should this be constructed for itineraries with several changes of carriers?

Nothing really new: According to an epigram of *Callimachus*: "Even the crows on the roofs caw about the nature of conditionals." [cit.: Kneale and Kneale 1971] The alternative recommended by probabilistic reasoning is obvious: Let us find calculation methods and possibility switches which can express the weakness of conclusions and allow multiple hypotheses to operate, in order to avoid major contradictions. A plausible solution is the introduction of low probabilities for exceptional cases, such as the ordering of decision branching according to entropy calculations. This approach is not only pragmatic because it takes all the lessons of common sense reasoning into consideration, but it also provides a practical algorithm for programming a problem. The pitfalls cannot be avoided: A really large-scale system, more complex by orders of magnitude than the usual paradigms (the Tweety case, the *Nixon-Republican-Quaker-Pacifist diamond*, the *Yale Shooting problem*, etc.) lead us quickly into a mess of complexity. In this case, anybody can say that the complexity is not infinite, that we can be much more fearless, having gigaflops and terabytes available. The difficulty grows, in spite of this immense computing power, due to the uncontrollability of uncertainty propagation. If we supposed that our Bayesian estimates are reliable statistical data received in accordance with all strict conditions of sampling, and add to these the data on distribution and confidence, then after very few consecutive steps of reasoning, we find how unreliable the whole will be. This ideal case of statistics never did exist, as we have emphasized several times—thus we can imagine how fragile all these logico-mathematical, probabilistic reasoning structures really are. A house of cards is a very lifelike metaphor (the edges of the cards can represent the branches of the decision tree). Nevertheless, it may be more stable than our weak reasoning.

This consideration is valid for any method, even those that can be theoretically wonderful and computationally manageable. *Circumscription* is one of them. Using higher order logic and embedded definitions, it expresses the exceptions in a generative way, providing a minimal model of the system. All birds can fly, except those whose wings are not appropriate for flying. This deficiency can be a feature of the species (penguin, ostrich, emu, cassowary) or due to abnormality (malady, injury, not alive).

CIRCUMSCRIPTION

We see that this kind of logical generative power is very different from the calculations of a mathematical model of the physical world, where we can obtain data which provide essentially new knowledge, new hypotheses, new devices.

Essentially different, but not completely! In both cases we have a basic model that is the result of all available data and works well. For people living in the Northern Hemisphere, all living, healthy birds could fly. For everyday life, similarly, Newtonian mechanics is perfect. New models are created either as a result of new, contradictory data (discovering the birds of the Southern Hemisphere, say, or measuring the velocity of light) or, less often, by rearranging existing data, i.e. discovering different models of the same situation. The latter is the case for, e.g., different religions. We can hardly recollect a change of a model produced by the generative power of the model *per se,* without additional external (external to the model's own closed world) information. Information that previously was consciously neglected can be considered as new data as well. As a hypothesis on the working of the system, a model is always a biased filtering of data considered relevant or irrelevant.

3.8 Causal or evidential?

 Similar considerations are due to the distinction between causal and evidential views. In practice we encounter a majority of cases that can be treated as causal relationships. The formulation is careful, according to our view, and this view is shared by many people working in epistemology. The concept of causal relationship is a human tool for representation of relationships (see the representation problem). It always supposes a transcendent force or will, whether it be God, Nature, or the System of Eternal Laws, that governs the consecutive history of events. "Do not be afraid to proclaim everywhere that God established these laws of nature just as a sovereign establishes laws in his kingdom ..." wrote *Descartes* in a letter to *Father Marin Mersenne* on April 15 in 1630.

The other view acknowledges interactions only. The paradigm of automata theory is an appropriate model for this, a hypothesis of basic atoms and interaction rules that generates the infinite variance. A major advance in this model is the possibility that new rules may emerge from the interaction of the offspring. It can be supposed further that these more complex rules are combinations of the original basic rules, just as the offspring are combinations of the atoms. The resemblance model used in particle physics and molecular genetics — in the basics of natural science — is similarly a model, a representation in the brain. Most probably there will never be a possibility of representing the Final Truth, a final decision on these two or other models. Nevertheless, this interaction scheme works and has less transcendental *Deus ex Machina* external assumptions than the others.

What does this mean for our computer models? We must be very careful in taking any relationship to be a causal one, i.e. a unidirectional, necessary consequence. The causal hypothesis is a very practical tool in reasoning, thanks to these two features. The unidirectionality is the stronger one; a possibilistic modality is a weaker variant. The unidirectionality hypothesis helps in the composition of a clearer, less ambiguous graph of events. Another cognitive reason for the success of the causal model is that causality fits our perception of events located on the time axis. This is really the popular chicken and egg problem, reborn in Artificial Intelligence!

The evidential view is closer to pattern concepts: a coincidence of events where the direction of effects cannot be predefined with certainty. This will be the subject of Chapter 5. Basically identical, these epistemological problems are reflected in any critical view of uncertainty, and therefore in any analysis of a recommended method, where the emphasis is on the strength of one or the weakness of the other. The circumscription approach is nonmonotonic (i.e. each extension can weaken the generality of consecutive causal relations) and nontransitive as well. This latter feature is dangerous for all automatic conclusions, all noncritical applications of inheritance relationships. We should not forget that inheritance is the backbone of our usual reasoning!

After this rather depressing roundtrip, we come back to our starting point: Logic is not an independent reasoning power. Its validity is most closely related to the certainty-uncertainty problem and therefore it can be treated and used only by recognizing this issue. Computer science, as a user of logic, is forced by all complex and responsible real-life applications to follow this rule. According to my knowledge, one of the best interpretations of these views has been provided by the probabilistic reasoning of *Pearl*.

Unfortunately this is not the end of the story. On the other hand there is language, the third mapping of reality. Logic somehow stands in a triangular relationship between and beyond the uncertainty of the external world and the delicate ambiguities of language as an attempt to express our internal world. These three issues are deeply interrelated, and our treatment, partitioning the subject into chapters and iterating similar topics in different paragraphs, reflects the poverty and confusion of our conceptual-modelling abilities. These remarks lead us to the next chapter on language. Before doing so, however, let us draw some preliminary conclusions which can justify the efforts of logicians over three millennia from the present, computer application viewpoint.

Is logic an epiphenomenon (a phenomenon not necessarily related to the basic nature of Reality)? This cannot be decided because it belongs to the Reality and Mind problem discussed in Chapter 5. However, just because of this reflective nature it must perform something relevant from the dynamics of the World. Similarly to the concepts, their relations are derivations, lower dimension views of the Universal Interactions, reflecting several important features, but most probably the Totality is hidden.

Logic is transformed *from* being the *structure* of processes *to* being their *scaffolding*. This means first, that in the continuous relationship of logic with language, logic advanced to take a primary role. The opulent development of logic provided a rich and computer-oriented expressive device, especially in its predicate structures. The success story of PROLOG is a nice demonstration of this role. It started with the claim of a general problem solver and could never accomplish this, but it became a very useful language for model building. The procedural, *syllogistic* power of logic is a workhorse of model testing, verification, and, if all runs smoothly, for actual usage. Logic's success in some areas

as a language can be termed phenomenal [Hopcroft, Ullman 1979].
Logic is, at least, both language and calculus, if not the philosopher's
stone.

TOWER ON SWAMP

"My mouth makes me comparable with men
My mouth gets me reckoned among men."
Babylonian cuneiform
W.G.Lambert: Babylonian Wisdom Literature,
The Clarendon Press, Oxford, 1960, p. 238.

Chapter 4
Language, the final representation

4.1 The mystery of language

The problems of epistemology—and of computer epistemology as well—start and end with language. Start, because language is like a mirror: It reflects knowledge in a form detached from our internal processes. As we look at this mirror, we encounter the similarities and differences between reality and our knowledge. The effort to model something, the epistemic procedure, also ends with language: The result is formulated in a linguistic way. *Language* is understood here *in a broad sense*, including natural language, mathematical formulae, or any means of communication and metacommunication. As we approach multi-media communication, integrating voice, sound, text, static and motion pictures in uniform digital media, we can and should look at this problem from the computer epistemological point of view, just as man has done during his entire civilization. Even more, this kind of communication of knowledge is more perfect than any previous ones, due to the very fast, mostly direct access, reliability of this access, and the possibility of multiple combinations and alternative pathways. But it can be misleading just because of the deceiving nature of those virtues. The access can be reliable, but not the information itself. It can be fascinatingly direct, and in real-time, but the feedback dialog is limited and sometimes these limitations are less obvious than would be the case in a face-to-face dialogue with a familiar person.

If something is deeply related to mysticism and this mystery repeatedly occurred several times in history in several forms and cultures, then there must be something extraordinary hidden within the issue. This must be particularly true if it is rooted in human behavior and not a distant externality, such as the other side of the Moon used to be before our time. *Genesis* starts with the same ranking of *Creation* and *Designation*, these were the twin origins of divine actions: "And God said, Let there be light and there was light. And God saw the light, that it was good. And God divided the light from the darkness. And God called the light Day, and the darkness He called Night" (*1:3-5*). Further, in *Proverbs*: "The preparations of the heart in man and the answer of the tongue, is from the Lord." (*16:1*). Or, in a very different culture: "What Buddha preaches in his language, people receive and assimilate in their own language as it was specially intended for them. Buddha's horizon surpasses human thought; it cannot be made clear by words or examples, it can only be hinted at in parables". (*The Teachings of Buddha, Bukkyo Dendo, Kyokai, 1966. p. 30.*) We could refer to a great number of similar citations, all of which express the basic paradox of communication that the mystique of language lies both in the possibility of human communication and in the impossibility of any perfection in that process. Any communication presupposes a tacit knowledge — as was pointed out by *Polányi* — i.e., the people communicating must have the same factual background knowledge, the same experiences, the same emotional attitudes, values, and interests. We encounter daily the impossibility of the ideal situation, whether between generations in the same family, between woman and man, or among people of different situations, cultures, status, national background, etc. *Johannes Scotus Erigena*, the great philosopher of the 9th Century wrote: "This stone or piece of wood means for me the light. And if you ask me how to understand, the intellect suggests to answer you: Observing that stone it reminds me to several issues which enlight my soul." On the other hand the miracle of art, as with *Buddha*'s preachings, is its open-ended nature. Nevertheless, *Goethe*, who reached a summit in the arts and was an optimist in final ends, said "the best of our conviction cannot be included into words. The language is not adapted for everything."

Wittgenstein, in his posthumus work [1953] shows how the meaning of a simple word is dependent on *family resemblance*, i.e. the relational knowledge of those people who have some connected experience, connected in both the use of the word and in experience related to a broader common environment. This family resemblance has *per se* no fixed borders, neither in the group of people, nor in the meaning at a certain time, nor in the time of the usage. How then can we put all these fuzzy limits into fixed frames and slots?

Quine [1961], a leading representative of classical logic, goes even further. He refers to the possibility of framing as "the myth of the museum." The interpretation, and therefore the representation, of a text is really a *polysemantic**, and therefore an ambiguous task of translation. This translation is also done by understanding a text written or spoken in the same language (language here in the ordinary, national language sense), a translation from the wording, expressions, conceptual world, logic, and patterns of the writer or speaker to those of the reader or audience.

---

* having several meanings

4.2 Anything human related — everything human related

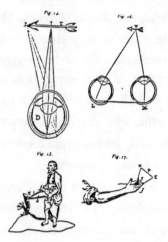

Anybody can argue that all these points can be valid for art, psychology, or human relationships but have nothing to do with computers and technology, where the objects, relationships, and processes are clear and well-defined. There really are relevant differences in the fuzziness of definitions of the standardized objects of industry compared to the social problems of people. If two robots cooperate in an assembly task in a closed environment containing only predefined objects, the communication is merely (?) a technical task. In these cases the problem is solvable, as was nicely demonstrated by the block world in the early days of Artificial Intelligence. You see that we have returned to the problem discussed in Section 3.5!

In more complex machine-to-machine communication tasks the problems will be tougher, as we observed in the development of the *OSI, ISDN* and *MAP protocols** and *standards*. These cases contain two difficulties. The first is the same as those of any very big software

---

* OSI, ISDN, MAP-TOP standards - These define interfaces of inhomogeneous systems of a certain but broad class of network usage. OSI (Open Systems Interconnection) is the most general one for all kinds of communication networks, defining 7 levels of cooperation interface. ISDN (Integrated Services Digital Network) is the protocol system for all kinds of digital communications (voice, picture, data). The MAP-TOP (Manufacturing Automation Protocol and the Technical and Operations Protocol) connects manufacturing equipment and business operations.

system, i.e. a high complexity of possible cases, states, which can go beyond any absolute control; the other is related more to the human background. Each component could interact and each interaction process has a history, a different definition, form, or usage in the history of the company, national standards, educational practices, etc. Concepts, priorities, and hierarchies of system definitions can hide company interests, such as the cost of rearrangements, reschedulings, redesigns, freedom for wider application, or limitations of usage, compulsions for a more expensive solution, etc. These biases can be discovered in every complex machine-to-machine communication protocol. They each have a linguistic, and, in consequence, a machine linguistic expression. This is far from a theoretical statement, constraints and compromises have far reaching and unforeseeable consequences in the form of contradictions, deadlocks, and dysfunctional blockages of further usage.

We were speaking about sterile machine-to-machine communication systems. The progress of Artificial Intelligence is directed toward those systems which contain, to a greater or lesser extent, human components. This relates not only to such areas as medical or legal applications, etc., but also to any organizational task such as, e.g. office automation, or any instance when a man is communicating with or operating machines. It is obvious that the problem increases with the extent of the human role; we can say that a task is more human, given the increasing possibility of ambiguities and unexpected complications. If these are equivalent to machine-machine communication problems, the task is completely inhuman!

4.3 Mind — language — logic

In this way, any linguistic communication problem is inseparably connected with social and psychological issues. Here we will emphasize this side of the complex as against the more usual computer-oriented view, looking at it from the standpoint of logic. This emphasis does not speak against the relationship of logic and language, rather it should only point to the other aspect, which is no less relevant, and of increasing significance due to the complexity of our systems and the spread of their applications. Further, we would like to hint at additional possible connections between the two aspects, looking at language from the internal, mind-direction and from the external (or believed external) standpoint, from logic.

Both views have a long history in human thinking and this is not mere chance. Language was the first objectively detectable and examinable stage of the four mappings of Reality. "Languages are the best mirrors of the human mind", according to *Leibniz*. We can extend the metaphor of a mirror by looking at the picture reflected: We do not know what distortions the mirror has or how well the photosensitive material reflects the shades and colors. *Aristotle*, in his (and most probably his group's) collected works later titled *Organon* (Tool), treated the logic (*Analitiké*), i.e. the ways of human thinking combined with linguistics. A portion of these epistemic Tools are devoted to problems of Meaning, semantics in *Hermeneutiké*. Logic, the mostly transcendentally understood Law of Reality, was related to the variable, subjective topic of meaning.

This view was also expressed by *John Stuart Mill*: "The principles and rules of grammar are the means by which the forms of languages are made to correspond with the universal forms of thought ... the structure of every sentence is a lesson in Logic."

This brilliant formulation builds not only a natural bridge between language and logic but helps in bridging alternative views on the relationship of grammar and the corpus of the language. According to *Chomsky*, a universal grammar should exist, somehow prewired in each human mind, independently of (or only slightly dependent on) the national language itself, a logical syntactic structure that serves as the skeleton of linguistic abilities. Other linguists deny this hypothesis and assign priority to the corpus (words, expressions). According to this latter theory, the structure is a more recent type of abstraction. Mill's view—in the mirror of recent assumptions in cognitive psychology—resolves this antagonism: The human brain's ontogenetic and phylogenetic physiological development and learning by socialization act in an orchestrated way to complete the developing status of our mind. The development of thinking structures is a long process of adaptation-learning-generalization. The structures of our cognition correspond to our adaptation-survival behavior experience, i.e. the reflection of external processes is crystallized in the logic of events and in syntactic rules for their representation. These considerations are relevant
for computer epistemology, they are not merely amusing speculations. We could say that AI is not too much more (or not too much less) than understanding and constructing languages for machines. Language is

understood in J. S. Mill's sense. This statement is even more valid if we can really establish a syntax-based semantic logic, i.e. the dynamics of the knowledge base (expressed by a language) should be equivalent to the inference engine. This ideal inference engine would contain natural (or quasi-natural) language understanding, learning, generalization, instantiation, and find or create analogies as well.

We return here from another side to the problem dealt with in Section 3.8, to the relation of logic (here language) to the real world's structures (here our mind's development in linguistic representation). The problems and relations are natural duals. How far this ideal inference engine should and will be analogous to our brain's activity, is an open question. It may never be answered. We get further in these considerations in Chapter 5. However, the endeavor of understanding these basic mechanisms helps us in two ways: How to do learning analogs, and learning the limitations of machine solutions.

4.4 Limited or unlimited — computable or amenable?

In this field, learning the human-biological lesson is not completely analogous with all other machine actions that were solved by avoiding the anthropomorphic or zoomorphic way, such as moving on wheels, flying by propeller or jet, etc. Solving or approximating the problem of human or animal intelligence requires that we understand the problem itself, just as we would first understand what moving or flying means. The analogies mentioned were trivial, but this problem is far from that.

This is a basic difference between designing a sterile, machine-machine communication and any other that contains human (inter)action in a direct or indirect way. It also expresses the difference between recent typical applications of computers as automata and artificial intelligence tasks, namely, that the human brain cannot be treated as or replaced by any kind of black box. This consideration affirms our earlier distinction about human and inhuman types of work.

Views on this subject are very different. Several claimants of original Artificial Intelligence perspectives, as well as some logicians and linguists, share the conviction that the range of these problems is limited and computable. Our considerations suggest the opposite hypothesis, that their range includes the infinity of the world and the infinity of reflections, among them possible states of mind and its expressive outputs. In modern times, in response to the arrogance of some Artificial Intelligence and Computer Science proponents, the *Dreyfus* brothers [1987] and *Putnam* [1975, 1981] have given an appropriate answer in this modest sense.

The modest standpoint is—maybe paradoxically—more research-oriented than the arrogant claims. The latter contend that they have possession of the solution and accordingly what is needed is nothing but more computer power, more investment in software, in data collection, and in system build-up.

If I were malicious, I would refer to *Swift*, to Gulliver's visit at the grand Academy of Lagado:

"We crossed a Walk to the other Part of the Academy where, as I have already said, the Projectors in speculative Learning resided.

The first Professor I saw was in a very large Room, with Forty Pupils about him. After Salutation, observing me to look earnestly upon a Frame which took up the greatest Part of both the Length and Breadth of the Room;

he said, perhaps I might wonder to see him employed in a Project for improving speculative Knowledge by practical and mechanical Operations. But the World would soon be sensible of its Usefulness; and he flattered himself, that a more noble exalted Thought never sprang in any other Man's Head. Every one knew how laborious the usual Method is of attaining to Arts and Sciences; whereas by his Contrivance, the most ignorant Person at a reasonable Charge, and with a little bodily Labour, may write books in Philosophy, Poetry, Politicks, Law, Mathematicks and Theology, without the least Assistance from Genius or Study.

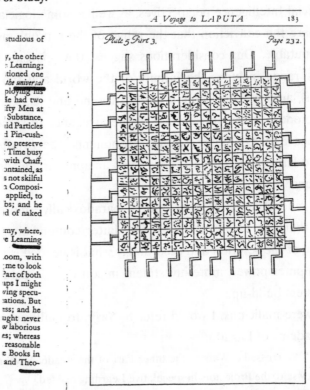

He then led me to the Frame, about the Sides whereof all his Pupils stood in Ranks. It was Twenty Foot square, placed in the Middle of the Room. The Superficies was composed of several Bits of Wood, about the Bigness of a Dye, but some larger than others. They were all linked together by slender Wires. These Bits of Wood were covered on every Square with Paper pasted on them; and on these Papers were written all the Words of their Language in their several Moods, Tenses, and Declensions, but without any Order. The Professor then desired me to observe, for he was going to set his Engine at work. The Pupils at his Command took each of them hold of an Iron Handle, whereof there were Forty fixed round the Edges of the Frame; and giving them a sudden Turn, the whole Disposition of the Words was entirely changed. He then commanded Six and Thirty of the Lads to read the several Lines softly as they appeared upon the Frame; and where they found three or four Words together than might make Part of a Sentence, they dictated to the four remaining Boys who were Scribes. This Work was repeated three or four Times, and at every Turn the Engine was so contrived, that the Words shifted into new Places, as the square Bits of Wood moved upside down.

Six Hours a-Day the young Students were employed in this Labour; and the Professor shewed me several Volumes in large Folio already collected of broken Sentences, which he intended to piece together; and out of those rich Materials to give the World a complete Body of all Arts and Sciences; which however might be still improved, and much expedited, if the Publick would raise a Fund for making and employing five Hundred such Frames in *Lagado* and oblige the Managers to contribute in common their several Collections.

He assured me, that this Invention had employed all his Thoughts from his Youth; that he had emptied the whole Vocabulary into his Frame and made the strictest Computation of the general Proportion there is in Books between the Numbers of Particles, Nouns, and Verbs, and other Parts of Speech."

Do not assume that this quotation resembles any recent, rumored mega-projects!

The other attitude indicates the open problems, encourages research in new directions, values hard, step-by-step progress. A relevant field of research is stimulated by this conduct: a search for limits, theoretical and practical ones, the latter related to available or reasonable resources, looking for ways around the problem, approximations, and compromises. This is one reason for our view as to why the acknowledgement of the limits of rationalism helps against the dominance of irrationalism.

As could easily be foreseen from the whole attitude of this book, our belief is in the open nature of natural language and the unsolvability of the problem of complete understanding of a natural language. For further reference, two quotations from the realm of those who rule over language with supreme authority: "If we know anything and see it by another method or even on another language, the subject makes an impression by the magic of novelty and fresh view" (*Goethe: Maxims and Reflections*). And, from a unique author, brilliant in two different languages, Russian and English, *V. Nabokov, On Translating Eugene Onegin*:

> "What is translation? On a platter
> A poet's pale and glaring head
> A parrot's screech, a monkey's chatter,
> And profanation of the dead."

Our belief is based on all previous considerations of the unlimited variety of complexity and especially on everything that is related to the human mind. We have seen the inexhaustible variety of the uncertainty issue and related that to the uncertainty of the concept itself. In this way we shall briefly dwell on one part of the linguistic problem: concepts.

4.5 Frail concepts

Concepts, and conceptual thinking, belong in the chapter on logic as well, since the entire reasoning process is based on generalization and instantiation by concepts. The idea of categories was the focus of ancient Greek philosophy and their treatment was very similar to our ideas of frames and semantic nets. The topos structures (locations) are hardly distinguishable from the slots or the **is a, part of** relationships, as it is illustrated by the table below.

Conceptualization
Aristotle — Frames (Minsky) — Semantic nets (Shank-Abelson)

τοπος	places (slots – dependencies)	e.g.
ουσια, τι εστι	substance (a priori)	bacteria
ποσον	quantity	10000/ccm
ποιον	quality	aerobic [intact]
προς τι	relation	parasitic [partly]
που	place	blood
ποτε	time	hour after sampling
κεισθαι	situation	in vitro
εχειν	possession	nuclei
ποιειν	action	multiply
πασχειν	passive state	passivated

Composition: one hour after sampling of blood 10000/ccm aerobic parasitic bacteria (were found) in vitro status multiplication (but) [partly] passivated with [intact] nuclei

If we wanted to be ironic, we could say that the only differences between the Greeks and recent AI authors are first, missing the claims of

Aristotle and the Stoics to have invented these ideas, and second, the more responsible and profound doubts of the classical thinkers about the ubiquity of these inventions. The paradoxes associated with the relationships of concepts and used by these intellectual pioneers are much more than games in logic—such deep thinkers of our age as *von Neumann* or the brilliant science writer *Hofstadter* are playing with this earnest tradition with similar elegance.

The pitfalls of conceptualization can be nicely demonstrated by a strange, but, from a certain point of view, quite feasible categorization, an old Chinese formula for animals (quoted by *J. L. Borges* in one of his short stories):

" – belonging to the Emperor
   – wild
   – look like a fly from a distance
   – can be depicted by a fine brush
   – all others."

Most relevant innovations start with a recategorization. This happens in the fields of natural science, technology, humanistics, and economics. One aspect of the fragility of categorization was treated in the chapter on uncertainty, related especially to the fuzzy concept, where the measure, membership in the conceptual entity, not the real value, is uncertain. This has a long history as well; one of the paradoxes collected (and not invented!) by *Eubulides* was the *Heap* or the *Bald*. The uncertain questions here, respectively, are: How long can we continue to take single grains from a heap before we no longer have a heap, and how many pieces of hair can somebody retain while still considered bald?

The power of conceptual thinking lies in the *inheritance* property. This is also the most shaky property as all examples of nonmonotonic logic demonstrate. Inheritance—mentioned several times earlier—is a strong relation of conceptual hierarchy. A more general concept owns attributes which are inherited by the instantiation, e.g. the old syllogism about the mortality of Socrates (the instantiation) being a man (general concept). However, Tweety does not inherit the flying ability from the General Bird. We can say that the fuzzy-like uncertainty above was the quantification part of conceptual weakness, but property inheritance is the qualitative part. These are the pivotal points for every case of decision making! The human experience, based on our own information and that received from others, makes decisions in a very different way from expert systems. This will be the subject of Chapter 5. Our problem is the estimation of these differences from two special points of view.

The first relates to the process itself. The human operation traditionally united the recipient of information, the decision makers, and the executors. In optimal cases, especially for a real specialist in the process, these phases were not strictly separated. He[*] worked in a continuous optimization manner, adapting abilities and processing them in a real-time, closed-loop operation. A critical processing of linguistic information was a relevant part of this harmonic procedure. Each time, as this harmony was disrupted and the continuity of interactions was broken, a critical situation arose.

Because these breakdowns occur frequently, a special network of *institutional responsibilities* was developed: organizational hierarchies, legal arrangements, professional ethics, etc. Each member of this net-

---

[*] A wonderful and terrible example of early linguistic conventions, of the name and names (Section 4.8) as well. The masculine (macho) society had one name only for human: Man. As a consequence, the pronoun *he* serves for general usage. Feminist revolution introduced the ugly he/she version (not, as would be more logical, a she/he one). Let us avoid this conflict here and hereafter by applying the traditional he and understanding by that first she and second he!

work had, and still has, a more or less well-defined competence for interpretation: God's commandments, the spirit of the Law, interests of nations or companies, the status of a sick person, or the operational conditions of a mechanism. We can reduce these vital professional functions, assignment of responsibilities, to conceptual interpretations. In this light we should consider the new responsibilities concerning a new situation when conceptualization, i.e. generalization and instantiation, happen by machine. In this case, the weaknesses of natural language, its imprecision, ambiguities, ellipsis, etc., are replaced by an artificial limitation of the infinite range of meaning. The limitation may be taken into account to some degree by the system design, but all possible consequences can never be foreseen nor can they be put under continuous control, in a similar fashion to the human operations outlined above.

All these lead us to the second point:

4.6 Meta

The apparent weakness in precision of natural languages (which is their strength in the arts) led to the idea of metalanguages, a language aimed at defining another language devoted to a certain subject. This can be understood by the procedure of a *negotiation*. First, let us define all that we are talking about and the ways we use these terms. The concepts surrounding metalanguages are as confused as many others leading to the exact meta-formulations.

Metaphysics for *Aristotle* is far from the terms' usage in later common colloquial language to refer to transcendental speculations, but originally it was a thorough, scientific attempt to find a logico-linguistic environment for descriptions of Nature. (The fact that the term Metaphysiké was later made the title of an ontological treatise that only denoted the book as next in sequence after physics is misleading.) The genuine meta concept returns, in a more or less covert way several times, especially in efforts representing a rationalist transcendental view. This view—which was, in some sense, both similar to and different from the common colloquial usage of metaphysics—supposed a transcendental, eternal structure, a Law of the Universe, as has been referred to several times in this essay. It was rational, because it had to be a well-formulated logical edifice, but it was also metaphysical, transcendental, because it considered this structure to be a truly superior, primary substance. Characteristic of this medieval metaphysical rationalism was the conceptual machine of *Raymond Lully* (c. 1236-1315), a Catalonian-Franciscan philosopher. It was made of seven superimposed disks that could be rotated about a common axis. Each disk had seven sectors on its rim and each sector was named by a concept. The rotation could construct hierarchical relationships and, in that way, all primitive concepts could be elevated to the divine level. The first AI machine! The other even much more ancient conceptual machine was the *I Ching* [Huang 1984] of the Chinese culture, an *Oracle* based on analogies, inheritance relations.

Similar but much more advanced were the efforts of *Leibniz* (in his *Theodicea*) and *Frege* in constructing a metalinguistic notational system which could describe the Laws of the Universe. All these were efforts to create a metalanguage, in any form, that could be a common and complete descriptor. This idea of Universal Law was the Ultimate Rationality, a complete and common descriptive system as a Universal Language and a General Logic which could be used as a *General Problem Solver* (let us recognize here as well the very recent but faded claims of *Newell* and *Simon,* or the noisy advertisements of the *Japanese Fifth Generation Computer* project!). These are all representations of the same viewpoint and the same endeavor. We see how the two metaconcepts, the transcendental and the rational-descriptive intersect.

The last attempt of this approach, Hilbert's work, started the revolution. *Hilbert* coined the concept of *metamathematics* in order·to build a Universe limited only to mathematics and create a metalanguage that did not belong to that closed Universe but enabled mathematicians to speak about mathematics, i.e. the outside edge of rigor. This effort finds a parallel in the work of *William of Ockham* 600 years earlier, as he tried to distinguish the Divine from the Real. The Gödelian revolution, stimulated by *Hilbert*'s agenda, has opened a new perspective: There is no closed world, no final representation. For computer science, this led to further results on noncomputability and nonsolvability problems for AI, and related efforts concerning the limits of representation.

In this way we have reached a new view of the metalanguage. It is not and cannot be a Universal Descriptor, the Grammar of the Universe independent of content, but, on the contrary, it must be a content and context dependent semantics, where syntax is a notational aid, and a collection of the permitted logical production rules. In that way, each branch of activity creates its own metalanguage, as communication protocols. Instead of being a Transcendent Device it became a pragmatic compromise, and in that way a very important, practical tool. The process is related to the phenomena described in Section 3.9.

As a result of compromises, the metalanguage takes an intermediate position between the subject and the language, and therefore this position can change its level. A computer language is a metalanguage from the point of view of a program, but each computer language must also have a meta, otherwise it is not understandable (the meta can be resident in the mind of a programmer specialist). A general language for all computer languages and their metas can be designed, especially for languages of the same breed, as was done by *D. E. Knuth* [1973]. No programming meta can do anything without a professional specialist metalanguage; this has long been understood in any professional activity which required communication-based responsible cooperative action, e.g. the military, all kinds of transportation, communication itself, law, commerce, etc.

The compromise in each metalanguage lies in the relativity of the closed world. They should represent and be represented by a closed world, i.e. a limited vocabulary, a fixed syntax, a limited number of production rules, exclusion of ambiguities, and any other complex structures, including the levels of conceptual hierarchies. On the other hand, it is and should be open-ended, capable of development beyond its minimal origin by the tacit knowledge of the user and the designer and extendible in unforeseen ways for future applications. For uniform parsing and understanding, the ideal would be a possibility for word-by-word interpretation. This can be done only in the most trivial cases. Even in regular computational programs this is not a viable requirement (I am not speaking here about general computer programs where computation has a minor role). The next step would be a sentence-by-sentence understanding, i.e. the avoidance of any external references. As we shall see in the next sections this also is difficult because of the naming-conceptual relationship. The ideal metalanguage should avoid embeddings, i.e. linguistic representations of higher order logic, semantic and semiotic references of intentions, situations, different worlds. From the parsing and control point of view the linear structure is ideal. We can see how limited we would be with a poor metalangauge and how many troubles, such as barely controllable loops, are to be expected by a really expressive, powerful one.

This is the practical point but for a more general argument we quote the philosopher *Nicolai Hartmann* [1950]: "From the point of view of categories, their autonomy towards each other is never so crucial, as is their context. Each isolation is secondary to their coherence and it appears frequently in *a posteriori* conceptualization."

The contradictions of fine tuning a conceptual form was clearly an issue for *Aristotle*, and it is still a lesson for us now: "We should not strive to achieve the same level of precision in each subject but in every case to such extent for the topic concerned which is permitted by the special nature of consideration. Because the carpenter and the geometer treat the rectangular in different ways: The first to that limit which is needed for his work, but the latter searches the substance or the substantial characteristic of the rectangle," and further, "the learned person is characterized by (the fact) that, he requires only as much precision in each problem as is permitted by the subject itself ..." (*Aristotle: Nichomachean Ethics, 1098/a-b*).

All these are far from calamities or are in any way dishonesties for computer science; they are even trivial for any application. We have only to abandon the exaggerated universal claims, arrogant forecasts, and extreme definitions. We should design our systems by a very critical and careful effort related to its linguistic requirements. These are the most important and most lasting interfaces of systems.

4.7 Transformations among linguistic representations

"Mirror, mirror on the wall,
Among the ladies in this land,
Who is the fairest of them all?"
It's me!
−K−

As we discriminate among natural language, metalanguage, and computer language, we are not only aware of the fact that these practical discriminations are and cannot be absolute definitions, but we are also inspired to look for their interconnections because a really intelligent man-machine system integrates all of them. Remarkable progress in linguistics and computer science − well-coordinated by mutual understanding − provides new perspectives. We do not intend to get into the details of these well-published works [Winograd and Flores 1986], but would like to suggest some aspects relevant to the objectives of this book.

The first relates to the representation problem. In practice, objects and relationships are represented from the different points of view of applications. A coin is a means of payment, but for adjusting a voltage switch on an electric shaver it is a tool, for balancing it can be a weight, for comparison a piece of metal, and for numismatics a work of art. This is the simple case, if the object's applications are separated. Nevertheless, in the human mind, all qualities are more or less present, retrieved only by the selective objective of application. The case is different for a device that has different applications, performs different functions, and therefore has differing representations within a cooperative process. A screw has a different representation for mechanical manufacturing, as a component in a catalog, in an order form, in an invoice, in the program of an automated storage system, on a design for assembly, in a robot control program to execute the assembly, and in an artist's sketch for advertisement of the whole device, where the screw is only a minor part.

These transformations of representations were once mostly carried out by people in an automatic way, especially if several parts of the process were done by the same individual. In those times, the warehouse was a shelf and the assembly robot a man, but he had to know which piece was required and where it was stored, where the center of gravity of the object was, where he could grasp it, in what direction he should turn it, etc. Last—but really not least, especially from our point of view—there was a person, a foreman, master, owner, or designer, who coordinated the whole process with a few instructions (even if he did it all himself), considering that all tacit knowledge about the different representations and their relationships is available to people. The problem of medical service is similar. A heart disorder has different pictorial representations in a textbook on anatomy, in tissue sections on slides, on an ultrasonic scanner, a computer tomograph, a nuclear magnetic resonance display, on a radiographic view, during open heart surgery, reflected in the waves of an EKG, or observing the auscultatory resonance with a stethoscope, etc. The synthesis is done in the practitioner's mind but this kind of operation, or something related to that, should be done by an automated system if the human interface is excluded from one or another of the steps.

The task of transformation and synthesis among representations is a hidden process within one individual but it is a linguistic task in any cooperative situation, as e.g. in the example above related to a surgical team. Some pictorial representations can be interfaced by geometrical transformations, but most probably this is only one part of the job due to the highly redundant information filtered and compressed by linguistic communication. The problem comes into the limelight in multimedia communication. As these new technologies advance and become more widely used in local and wide area networks, new approaches are need-ed for intelligent representation interfaces, standard methods for the exchange of pictorial and linguistic morphological information, and this should be a commutative and transitive solution — as far as possible and with well-defined limitations and warnings.

4.8 Name and named — de dicto — de re

A slightly different aspect of the linguistic problem is the an-cient ambiguity of the *de dicto — de re* issue. This is a part of the mystery of conceptualization. Remember the way God did it: "And ... the Lord God ... brought them unto Adam to see what he would call them: and whatsoever Adam called every living creature, that was the name thereof." (*Genesis, 2:19*) Philosophy started with *Plato*'s concept of the *idea* and has followed that concept through its entire history. We shall come back to the psychological origins of this concept in Chapter 5, but it should be men-tioned here as well for the linguistic-logical aspect. We name an object, a subject, a relation, or any group of those which are factual and unique, individual entities. The name as a concept immediately starts to have a semi-independent life in our thinking and in our colloquial language, but the real entity continues its regular life after the naming. I may refer to *Daisy Deer* as my sister-in-law, but after my divorce, she will no longer be so, while I may have two other sisters-in-law. But the original text and reference remains; there is no continuous updating mechanism, be-cause complex entities and complex relationships never have a closed-world feature, neither in relationships, nor in time. This is a further

practical hint for interface design: The simple example given also
creates difficulties as interfacing, the separation of name and entity
should cause external changes only in this case. We find a very common
programming problem as a new appearance of a very old phenomenon:
"But the name is a copy, similar to a picture" (*Plato: Cratylus 431a*).

4.9 Linguistic encounter of different worlds

A similar consideration leads us to
our last specific comment: the
problem of low quality, imperfect,
defective information. This is related in some fashion to the issue
above: The human actor adds all
the peripheral information, the
tacit knowledge, to his decisions; the information exchange is based on
this mutual supposition by both sides.

There are minimum three-world problems, an illustration of which
is found in Section 3.3. Two are those of each of the communicating actors and the third is the world of the subject. Typical examples are: the
salesman, the customer, and the item on sale; the lawyer, the client, and
the case; the doctor, the patient, and the illness, etc. Each actor and
subject have different models in the minds of the other actors, and different linguistic and metalinguistic representations. (Attention! The
metacommunication is referred to here in its usual meaning, i.e. all
kinds of communication beyond the verbal, and has nothing to do with a
metalanguage as discussed in Section 4.6. We unconsciously meet here
a nice example of languages of different worlds' languages!)

Human experience — formulated from this point of view — is possession of a large number of models, actors and cases, as well as the ability
to do matching, transformation, and composition among them. As we
see, in this sense the problem is similar to the multiworld/multi-
representation task discussed above but even more complex. We could
here follow the somewhat hierarchical manifold of uncertainty, of logical inconsistency, nonmonotonic behavior of multiworld systems, and
the difficulties of linguistic interfaces among those uncertain, incomplete, but different worlds. Behind all that we see anywhere lies the
eternal dichotomy of model (in mind, text, or computer) and Reality,
the need for switching between different worlds. This was *Montague*'s
problem of the existence of intensional worlds.

What kind of concluding practical advice could be given? The first
one relates to the overall context: The management of uncertainty, logical reasoning, and language cannot be separated. *Konolige*'s [1985] requirement of a consequential closure, or, approximately the same concept, *Hintikka*'s [1973] *logical omniscience*, are those ideals that cannot
be satisfied in any more complex, practical problems. The paradigm of
different worlds, discussed first in Section 3.3, reappears several times in
our considerations, these worlds being rather indefinite, fuzzy compartments of an unlimited universe. Object-oriented programming, fine distinctions between objects and classes, more or less consolidated conceptual and procedural environments with islands, agents between
them, flexibly defined flavors, all are representation tools for these practical problems. A careful design, a skilled use of these and other varied
practical methods is needed, without messianic belief in any of them.

The life-cycle of the system should be closely followed, since any change in the supposed or real environment, any apparently slight adaptation or enhancement can modify the relationships, the assumed borders, and the interactions of those world compartments.

Chapter 5
Patterns and cognitive psychology

5.1 Rational-irrational — encore

We have followed several kinds of weaknesses in those devices that were the proud achievements of human thinking. This progress was particularly related to the European culture's style of philosophy and natural science, originating with the ancient Greeks more than 2.5 millennia ago. We have tried to indicate that these weaknesses were, on the whole, familiar to those who first used these epistemic instruments; those who later claimed to reinvent them often forgot to refer to them. These weaknesses or inconsistencies became apparent in our days as they began to be used as practical, widespread methods of computing. The extent of the systems analyzed, built, and controlled by these methods has outgrown the scope of simple human control.

Nevertheless we cannot emphasize enough that all these methods, in spite of their intrinsic problems, are admirable achievements of human progress. They have helped to increase our power to defeat famine, cold, disease, and distance — we are speaking about real positive achievements. If we look further from this height, it is done entirely in the sense of this book: Scientific responsibility and a self-respect should be one of its highest virtues: A critical viewpoint, a knowledge of presently existing limits is a stimulus for further research, an admonition for a conscious modesty (which should not be confused with the hypocritical pseudo-modesty that was an obligatory attitude in some societies). A clear view of these achievements and limits is the best weapon against that kind of irrationalism and mysticism which leads societies into dangerous adventures, as has been done several times during our century. This view can be the best way of avoiding the irrational exaggerations of the antitechnology movements as well.

The problems of the logico-mathematical artifacts led to a return to investigation of the human mind's performance.

5.2 The hype of intellectual omnipotence

The new approach is characterized by the abandoning of two historical hypes. The first was the claim for a real artificial intelligence, i.e. a machine that could function in the same way as a human brain, perhaps even better. This has been referred to several times in this book: the belief in the possibility of a mechanical (electronic) reproduction of the human brain. This view contained two further hypotheses: First, the idea that the human brain can fully understand and describe the human brain, including all its activities. Second, the expectation that improved mechanical and electronic components can then imitate those activities.

The former is due to the first human intellectual revolution: an unwillingness to accept the world as it is. Civilization started a revolt against Destiny, and therefore endeavored to understand the logic of events and build a speculative structure for reconstruction and prediction. The long-held belief in the omnipotence of logic lies in this endeavor. This is the reason why the tendency was so entrenched, in spite of all the new discoveries and different ideologies.

The metaphor of *Jacob*'s two dreams has reappeared in different forms in the ideologies of different ages. The first (*Genesis, 28*) was the "ladder set up on the earth, and the top of it reached the heavens: and behold the angels of God ascending and descending on it." The second dream (*Genesis, 32*) is the struggle with the Angel of God. As a result "the hollow of Jacob's thigh was strained," but he was blessed "for thou hast striven with God and with men, and hast prevailed." The dream and struggle of Jacob with God returned in different forms in the ideologies of different ages. Ancient philosophy was mostly directed towards an earthly world while the logicians of the Middle Ages were heaven-oriented, but the difference was only in the point of attack and the strategy — Platonic unification or the attempted detachment of *William of Ockham*. The Age of Reason presented magnificent attempts at a unification strategy by *Newton* and *Leibniz*, who both created a rational theology based on natural science. Jacob's dream tempted the greatest personalities of modern science as well, like *Einstein, Heisenberg* or *Monod*, to mention only a few.

The basic idea has always recurred: *Find a few atomic components and a few basic rules of composition and try to reconstruct the world from these bricks and mortar.* There is no real difference between the seemingly primitive views of the primary elements and modern science's views in molecular biology and particle physics. The lessons of complexity were

somehow suppressed as a Freudian psychological evil. *Goethe* was aware
of this:

> "This is the quality of matter
>
> For what is natural, scarce the world has place;
>
> What is artificial, needs restricted space."

Each new technology and technology-related scientific advance supported these beliefs. In ancient Greece, geometry played this role, as a
device which could help in the construction of buildings, or assist in
navigation. Mathematical analysis and clockwork automata were the
next major steps, and now electronics and computer science have assumed a similar role.

This hype was sometimes a stimulus for research and technology in
several directions, but there was an implicit bias in approaches to the
problem: It was based on an unrealistically simplistic model and con-
centrated efforts on the verification of this model. A research project
may and should have some models as hypotheses, but it must have an
ability to deviate from these models or even abandon them completely.
In my opinion (which is a hypothesis as well) this model is a *perpetuum
mobile* theme of epistemology. We quote only two recent examples: the
claim for the possibility of a complete decoding of human genetic
material, and by that the understanding of the human genesis, creating a
new Homunculus and neural nets as the last word in artificial intelligence, understanding the brain's mechanism and creating an artificial brain.

5.3 The hype of human exclusivity

The other hype was, in some sense, the opposite, while in another sense the consequence of the first. It was essentially a hypothesis of the divine nature of mankind, a sharp separation of the human intellect from any other biological development. The idea is well-described in the Bible: "And God said, Let us make man in our image, after our likeness: and let them have dominion over the fish of the sea, over the fowl of the air, and over the cattle, and over all the earth, and over every creeping thing that creepeth upon the earth." (*Genesis, 1:26*) The long history of this idea took on a new light in the Age of Reason as philosophers started to reconsider new aspects of the first hype: the relationship between man and machine. *Descartes* — by practically inventing the celebrated *Turing*-test — argued that the difference between animals and man is just this possibility of recreating every animal's brain as a machine, but that the divine nature of man lies in the impossibility of a similar mechanization of the human brain. The prevalence of logical and other well-formed structures in Artificial Intelligence were later reflections of this separation of human ways of thinking, giving a natural priority to performances that were considered specifically human. This human bias was an inhibition in looking for all the evolutionary aspects of intelligence; it simultaneously limited efforts to a smaller area of mental phenomena, and logically to those which could be treated by the available mathematical methods.

As research in *ethology* and *cognition* progressed this hope started to melt. People proved that the highest level of representation, the representation of self, is also present in some animals. The lack of this level had been the final argument for man's essential mental dissimilarity from animals. A chimpanzee who had learned about mirrors had a mark painted on his face during a dormant period. He recognized the change in the mirror immediately, and started to get rid of the mark based on the image. He was aware of the fact that he looked at himself in the mirror.

Ethology and developmental neurology have recently delivered several new results which can no longer be neglected.

5.4 Learn the cognition of phylogeny!

All these reconsiderations led to a more unbiased approach, one that lets us see how animals and humans learn the experimental lessons of *cognitive psychology* and the study of biological evolution. This new discernment was not only dissimilar to previous ones in its objective: It did not attempt to imitate nature but learn from it, i.e. to enhance existing knowledge and ideas with those that could be applied in direct and indirect ways.

Relationships between mind and computer, experimental results about cognitive processes in animals and humans now have an abundant and excellent literature; several schools are fighting each other, mostly on those issues which are very difficult to decide. In the experimental field, this relates to those problems of uncertainty and statistics which were discussed here as well, i.e. the difficulty of having a sufficient number of cases, the barely decidable method of classification, clustering, and the measurement problem itself. This last is special for psychology, since direct measures practically never exist. Indirect parameters for characteristics of performance are baised *per se,* as a logical consequence of some hypothetical reaction model. The field is dominated by such hypothetical models, especially those dealing with conditioning: How are behavioral phenomena conditioned by an inherited phylogenetic development, how is that in turn conditioned by socialization (the problem is similar for animals), and how are both related to instantaneous behavior by an individual? This is no criticism. It reflects the essential nature of the situation; it stems from the problem itself. Responsible scientists are aware of that and try to see their own results from these critical points of view. We may only draw attention to the special, innate features of this general problem with respect to the cognition field: Remember *J. S. Mill*'s metaphor about the mirrors! In spite of all, much has already been done which can be applied in an appropriate way, and this is one of the most challenging research areas for the future.

It is beyond the objectives of this book to give a survey of the state of the art in this area; this can be found in the current literature and textbooks on cognitive psychology[*]. We shall dwell on only a few points which are related to our concerns and practices. It will surely be a subjective selection on a subjective issue.

After the denial of a biased, hypothetical approach, we must enter the trap we promised to avoid. The hypothesis we will discuss relates to the phylogenetic development of the neural system, its methods and motivations. Let us start, however, with some facts which can be surprising for a computer addict but are everyday trivialities for any child living in a natural environment.

------

[*] [Tversky 1962; Allport 1980; Fodor 1983; Pylyshyn 1984; Bechtel 1988; Mérő 1990]

Anybody can admire those intelligent behaviors of animals which are evidence of their high-level adaptation, learning, action planning abilities. The orientation of insects, e.g. bees, is based primarily on the direction of the sun's rays, but it also takes the elapsed time into account in a manner similar to a precise computer. This capability is enhanced by a search strategy. Birds have an extremely high-level, complex orientation ability, and rats can memorize very complicated mazes. Recognition, distinguishing between edible, healing, and poisonous material is much better in several kinds of animals than in humans. Predatory activity requires sharp recognition, adaptive search, pursuit, and fighting strategies, a knowledge of the prey's behavior, anatomical weaknesses, and, with some species, social behavior and cooperation as well.

We have similar examples in lower level animals as well. If a small paradise fish is put in an aquarium with a bigger one, it swims around the predator, learning its behavior; if it does not appear dangerous, the smaller fish follows its normal activity, if there is danger, it escapes [Csányi 1985]. Social behavior in higher orders of mammals, especially primates, provided many surprising antecedents for existing and still dominant human attitudes. Over the last decades, biology has supplied additional important lessons on the once mythical, later underestimated, complex story and nature of intelligence. The most primitive organisms have a primordial component of memory and of changes in status, just as in computers where a single bit can be a stored information as well as a flag for bifurcation [Csányi 1988]. The earlier, static view of the genome is changing now; it has its dynamic, variational possibilities, the capability for interaction. These variational-interaction processes are the basis of adaptation, a dynamic of survival; they provide a model for all further high-level structures and procedures, including the human brain, and agrees well with the findings of brain research, as will be noted in Section 5.7.

At the beginning of this century, psychology discovered the same facts in its top-down manner. (According to our computer science metaphors we consider brain neurology research as a bottom-up approach.) *Gestalt* was the German word coined by *Ehrenfels* for the phenomenon of overall pattern, shape, form, appearance, contour, design, figure, frame, arrangement. It refers to mental entities that are composed of lower organized elements but somehow work together, each component changing its individual behavior within the particular composition. The same idea is covered by such words as pattern, scheme, and many others. Different disciplines reach similar conclusions with different names in a similar way. The application of *The Gestaltist look* is similarly not a new idea in Artificial Intelligence either. Minsky and Papert in 1973 summarized their earlier positive considerations on the topic. Later *Fu* [1983] published some proposals on the subject. *Gelsema* and *Kanal* [1988] organized a special symposium on this integration.

For our present purposes, it is irrelevant to make further hypotheses on brain structures. We remain somewhere near *Putnam*'s formulation: "The mind and the world jointly make up the mind and the world," or *Goethe*'s quotation in Section 3.2. This is valid for the nature of a man-machine world as well. By estimating possibilities about the impossibility of machine substitutions for humans, we are looking for inspiring analogies and hope to see what we can do with present instruments, using these analogies. The triangle of machine pattern recognition, the lessons of animal and of human perception can fill some gaps in the mathematics of uncertainty, logic, and linguistic communication. This is another reason why we will not enter into detail on those results in cognitive psychology and computer-related sciences which anybody can find elsewhere.

5.5 The trinity of patterns

As in every epistemological issue, we encounter several different but related conceptual frameworks, the relation among which is the fundamental theoretical and practical question. Pattern is a reality of the Universe, as in a constellation of stars, the shape of a snowflake, the landscape of human activity, or the collision trajectories of elementary particles. A further class of patterns is something which reflects those natural patterns in our minds, truncated and enhanced by brain activity, i.e. filtered in memory, joined to other patterns stored in the brain, etc. Lastly, they are communicated in a linguistic, program-oriented form, a transformation which needs a further essential brain activity, e.g. generalization, conceptualization, value estimation, and fitting them into the Procrustian bed of existing frameworks of expression (concepts, words, numbers, etc.).

According to the definition given by *Ludwig Fleck* (a philosopher of science and cognitive psychologist in the 1930s): "The Gestalt is not constructed of objective physical components but of cultural and historical motifs." [Fleck 1983]. This remark narrows down our concept of patterns, but it reflects a relativity referenced to the human mind, i.e. the second appearance of the pattern in our senses. This seemingly unnecessary iteration of the transformation process illuminates the fact that conceptually we find in it no novelty. The Platonic views of ideas, the mystical cabbalistic views on the secret coherences of events, and the rationalist Aristotelean-Thomistic-Cartesian thought processes attack the same issue [Dreyfus 1988], of course, from different aspects and with varied success. Nevertheless, two major additions can be noted in the recent past. The first is the mathematical and computational apparatus of pattern recognition, the second is the lesson of the above-mentioned observations on animal and human cognitive behavior. In combination, these have created the possibility of a weak, analogy-based approach for computer science and achieved a forced retreat of ideological barriers.

Ideas about cognitive relationships are evidently ancient. *Ibn Sina* (Avicenna), the great philosopher and physicist of Arabic culture, classified the steps of mental cognition processes in a way similar to modern science: sensory input, creation of an image, identification of the image with concepts, grouping these concepts (conceptual frames), evaluation, reasoning, decision, and storage of experience. He was aware of the fact that, to a greater or lesser extent, animals have the same cognitive abilities. The emphasis on image (pattern) is very instructive for us — after a thousand years! We have to add that *Ibn Sina* had, according to several Latin translations, a more profound effect on European thinking than even *Ibn Rusd* (Averroes), but in having so significant a role he must have had a long sequence of predecessors in addition to his own contributions. Another lesson, following this Arabic-medieval line, is the mixture of these deep and far reaching ideas with mysticism. This is the realm of Reality which we in the West today qualify as Uncertainty; the basic difference in our views lies in the attitude with which we look at such areas. Quoting *Wittgenstein*: "Not *how* is the World is the Mystical but *that* it is." (*Tractatus, 6.44*)

5.6 Intuition and memory

 A relevant perception of human reasoning methods was the experimentally proved fact that even professional people do not infer according to the laws of probability. People hardly conditionalize as the Bayesian theory would suggest; estimates on beliefs are biased towards extremes, subjective logical conclusions do not coincide with the elementary rules of logic and probability (e.g. additivity of independent or exclusive events, etc.). Most human judgements are partly influenced heavily by very recent experiences or impressions and partly made without such influence, especially if they are not emotional but conservative in the sense that they reflect experience of past conditions. Visual illusions are only one phenomenon of our more general cognitive illusions. In primitive peoples this pattern-driven thinking is more apparent. To quote from a study of uneducated gypsies: "Their thinking is picturesque, frequently broken into mosaics."

These were lessons for a critical view of human judgement, even when performed by good professionals. *Tversky's* [1974] group made several experiments with professional people and the results resembled those of the uneducated. On the other hand, we have an incentive to look for other reasons why either of these more or less experienced people are still mostly better than our theoretically correct algorithms.

"It was a 'home variant.' I caught the view of the motive and the mate pattern was familiar" – said the 13-year-old *Judit Polgár,* the Hungarian chess phenomenon, at the finals of the Saloniki women's Olympic Chess Games which she won in 17 moves, sacrificing a queen and knight in a situation seen otherwise as lost. The three *Polgár* girls who won the well-deserved admiration of the chess world were carefully educated for success, having a chess library of several thousand books at home and learning the patterns they contained. All interviews with chess masters tend to show similar results; especially convincing is one with Kasparov. He said and proved that he has about the same number of chess situations in his memory as he has words.

The same experience can be found in confessions of great mathematicians, although such activities as chess and mathematics are considered the two closest to logic. Most remarkable is the story of the ingenious autodidact and Indian mathematician *Shrinivasa Aiangar Ramanudjan* (1887-1920) who had an eidetic (photographic) memory and who claimed to achieve his fantastic discoveries in number theory and analysis from suggestions made during his dreams by the God *Namagiri*. Even in other fields, where the fundamentals are not arbitrarily created by humans (as are chess pieces or move definitions, axioms of mathematics, rules, proof methods, and theorems), humans confirm even more strongly the relevance and priority of these nonlogical intuitive mechanisms. "Invention is not a product of logical thinking but much more of intuition," was the opinion of *Einstein*. And in the views of many authentic experts in Artificial Intelligence, including such notables as *Marvin Minsky*: "Thinking always begins with suggestive but imperfect plans and images, these are progressively replaced by better – but usually still imperfect – ideas;" or *J. Pearl*: "The word *discovery* carries with it an aura of mystery because it is normally attached to mental processes that leave no 'memory' trace of their intermediate steps."

It seems to be a general ability of living organisms to store a pattern of situations which are relevant for survival. The more advanced the organism is, the more extensive is the ability. This extension is reflected in the number of possible variations of the nature of the pat-

reflected in the number of possible variations of the nature of the patterns and in the sheer number of them. (The latter is not so simple either, because it is rather difficult to define what a single pattern is, or how a single variation deviates.) Cognitive psychologists found that for any practical use, a low but adequate number is about 2000 (Chinese characters, basic words, concepts of a profession, etc.) and the highest art of a profession is characterized by about a few tens of thousands of patterns. How much and to what extent all that is predetermined, "prewired", and what about it may be changeable (learnable), is a challenging problem as well. This is investigated in different dimensions: inheritance, learning during a certain period of life and being fixed thereafter, open memory, mixtures of the above, and interrelations of the same issues with a slight analogy to read only, read mostly, random access, and cache memory of computers. The analogy can be carried further: preset files, procedural components in hardware, etc.

The other dimension is the relationship between development (phylogenetic as well as ontogenetic) and acquisition of skills in real time. There should be a prepared ensemble of components of different complexity, as we have in our VLSI design, in a cell library. This is the way children progress in their thinking from definite objects, items, towards symbolic thinking by concepts, according to the investigations of *Piaget* and those of his followers who refined these observations. In computer science we do things in a similar way, starting by programming from elementary code, and progressing towards higher and higher level languages and symbolic computation. Nevertheless, this thought process is not unidirectional. Beyond the highest level of sublime symbolic thinking, we find prototypical representations of a single item. The concept *mother* is represented by our own parent, *women* by a beloved (or hated) single instance, and a sitting situation is related to a certain chair, etc.

These fixed and combination structures are sources of strength and weakness at the same time: While they offer an ability to build in an immediate reaction, they also create the trap of a fixed yet inadequate response. A good example of the latter was the Japanese use of Katakana symbols for foreign language transcripts. These were developed to enhance Chinese characters with agglutination symbols (not necessary for the Chinese language), but the symbols do not adequately cover the syllables of Indo-European languages. This may be one reason why some Japanese speak foreign languages in a strange way. Nevertheless, very few people can learn another language without an accent after their teenage period. The reason is similar: All vocal patterns of articulation are set by learning once this age-level is reached. These patterns are extremely complex muscular and neural formation primitives and patterns. Later, people may adopt styles of speaking patterns to help them communicate within their own community, but it is always funny if someone uses, for example, the speaking style of a preacher at a jolly juvenile party.

Differences in orders of magnitude among those components (as we have seen in patterns of human experience) reflect the need for so large a reservoir in a creative, innovative adaptation.

5.7 Distributed and dynamic

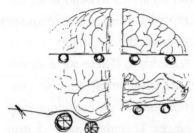 Brain research has proved the phylogeny of this complexity. They discovered first that certain parts of the brain are responsible for different basic activities, such as vision, memory, etc. Later it was found that this picture is much more complex. The brain acts as a distributed, cooperative system of more elementary functions. Vision, for example, is a process distributed among edge detection, motion sensing, color identification, etc., utilizing memory for faces, names, numbers, etc.* We experience this in our everyday practice, as we remember the initial of a name but not the full name, or in how we can strengthen some of our memorizing abilities, such as secretaries remembering telephone numbers, haematologists blood data, and radiologists individual X-ray pictures of patients — some may be recognized after several years on the basis of data particular to the person in question. On the other hand, we can lose the memory, or the pointers to it, due to lack of practice or aging. Most probably, all these basic functional components of the brain were separate, single reactive elements of primitive neural systems. Man and his higher level animal relatives merged these into a highly flexible, rich organization of instrumental variety.

The different ways of thinking are generally not in contradiction; they are well-coordinated in a creative brain. Psychology experiments

---

* [Hubel and Wiesel 1979; Julesz 1981; Marr 1985]

have proved that these brain activities are mostly not separated in distinct phases but work in continuous interaction.

Szentágothai [1975, 1983], *Edelman* [1978] and *Eccles* [1976, 1980] developed a rather complete model of this modular development and interaction. The neuron structures, according to the microscopic evidence of anatomy, are organized structures of several thousand internally and externally coupled bundles. These interactions are accomplished by chemical and electric means. Some are direct, connecting several neurons, while some have distinctive environmental effects. The hypothesis, based on strong evidence, states that these structures and connections correspond to those formations we call patterns. These bundles and connections are highly redundant at one phase of embryonic development. Further development is partly defined by the genetic heritage, but is also partly free to evolve depending on their excitation. The process is somehow analogous with the way we imagine the statics and the dynamics of patterns themselves.

In this way we have strong evidence that the models (patterns) *and procedures* (dynamics of patterns) can be localized in the brain and have a physiological mapping. Previous statements of our concerns are affirmed by a physiological proof of different representation phases for a concept in the brain and for another phase, the linguistic representation, which fires the motor functions of speech. Further, EEG waves can clearly indicate a difference in the brain process of identifying the same word in a written text as either a noun or as a verb. Similar experimental results show much the same phenomena with cats and chimpanzees: distinct phases and functions of sensing, processing (thinking!), and performing actions. The brain was developed by and for patterns and their dynamics!

One more lesson. *Donald Michie*, a distinguished AI pioneer, offered the following as a consolation: Our hardware may be deteriorating
but software will be richer. Patterns are handled in a dynamic way.
They are dynamic – according to some results and hypotheses of psychology – in certain respects. (A distant analogy could be the mobile existence
of elementary particles, a complementary dualism of motion and location in space and time.) This dynamic nature of patterns has its own patterns as well. This is what we feel through common sense reasoning,
finding relationships and analogies. How the dynamic structure is related
to the stored memory pattern remains hidden; we have experienced structures created by nature that are much beyond the single-function level
of the mechanical-electrical devices that serve us as miserable instruments and analogies. This means that static and dynamic pattern behavior is probably not strictly separated and has manifold possibilities both
similar and different for each pattern type and each pattern of recognition in a brain. Patterns of the mind are in some sense living organisms,
and brain research has discovered several interesting dynamic features
quite different from the engineering analogs.

5.8 Expert systems and patterns, why not trivial?

After these lessons, we can return to our problems in the artificial realm. Expert systems started with an uncertain confession of the failure of original artificial intelligence claims. Instead of having a fully automatic system that operates on input data, and rules flavored only by some mathematically correct, predefined heuristics, expert systems used human experience both for estimating data and for reasoning. This means that essential ingredients of earlier AI constructs play only a superficial role. MYCIN itself, as the most elaborated prototype, reflects, to a much greater extent than any previous developments in computer science, these concerns with human ways of thinking outlined above.

The application of patterns is a further logical step, a bit similar to the extension of single-parameter control systems toward multivariable structures. This was apparently a predictable step, since many people started to take it in developing expert systems; nevertheless the process was very slow and cautious [Fu 1983; Waterman 1978; Gelsema 1988]. Many systems concerned with the application of patterns use statistics only as a data processing enhancement, several others apply prefabricated boxes, e.g., frames for concepts, that are far from the lessons learned from cognition.

This remark is intended not as a criticism but as a diagnosis of some essential difficulties. In a linear control system, which was our earlier analog for more complex actions, we substitute vectors and matrices for scalars but the whole structure remains similar. Behind the matrices, however, we find an increasing computational complexity. Because of that and due to basic uncertainties, we get truncation errors, and increased uncertainty in the whole model. Patterns can still be handled less than adequately in that way, or they can diverge very far from the reality.

The major problem lies in two related issues: The first is the difficulty in expressing by a single value the manifold of values contained in a pattern. This singular, scalar value is needed for further reasoning steps, such as decision making, otherwise the system would collapse with an unmanageable multitude of branchings. The second problem is the metric of these values. This issue is similar to those which are discussed under the uncertainty heading and is related to semantics. Let us consider fuzzy estimation. A statement on membership value, e.g. between 0.65-0.8, contains a certain relationship to other parameters of the pattern, as we discussed in Section 2.5. A statement about somebody being moderately tall depends on age, sex, geographical region, and historical time, etc. The fuzzy metric expressing this verbal statement in numerical data takes these relationships into account. For this reason and many others, the metric is nonlinear in most cases (e.g. most of our sensory impressions and many natural processes are logarithmic or follow other nonlinear characteristics according to the *Weber-Fechner* resp. *Stevens*-Law) [Mérő], nonuniform, and, in the decision of space, dependently variable on time and context.

These are the very reasons why most systems which are aware of the importance of the pattern view, do not really use the deep pattern concept. The problem of metric is intrapattern and interpattern as well, it concerns the creation of patterns and the relations of them, i.e. contexts, hierarchies, etc.

5.9 Metric—the kernel of the pattern method

For the execution of computing tasks, we possess algorithmic procedures which have been developed in the long and fruitful evolution of pattern recognition, and which are based on the mathematical results of estimation theories. Anticipating our further remarks on neural computing, these procedures offer new implementation challenges but, until now, not too much has come from this basic aspect. As we shall see, this remark is not a qualification; the challenge can be just as great from those aspects that do not have much mathematical novelty.

What kind of procedure can be recommended? The first step should be—as is the rule for any knowledge-based system—to interview an expert in the domain about his professional patterns. For example, in the medical field a pattern is a *syndrome*. (The Greek word is very expressive: Items *running together*, which is an archetype of patterns; it can contain all kinds of phenomena, visual, audio, tactile, smell, laboratory measurements, anamnestic data, time variances, etc.) Furthermore, a pattern will later be related to a diagnosis or a complex treatment. In legal practice, the pattern is a case description with a heading describing the evidential or proved charge (e.g. murder, robbery, insult to privacy, etc.), statements on a situation (e.g. custody, divorce, bankruptcy, etc.); all circumstances which are or should be considered in a judgement (e.g. social and mental status, age, intention, cooperation, social threat, etc.) are ingredients of the pattern. Any medical or legal textbook on cases and materials is organized in a similar way. The difficulty starts with the multitude of special, irregular cases which are the art of professional excellence (remember the 2000 vs. 50000 patterns) and the above mentioned riddle of a proper metric.

From the computational point of view, a pattern is a set (record, file) of data, with procedures related to them, and some linguistic structures. The closest idea in software is the object or the class in the sense used by the SMALLTALK (earlier SIMULA) language and in the implementations of the descendents of these languages.

If a standard professional metric does not exist — and this is the case for most problems — then one would be advised to allow an experimentation period. As is apparent, a metric understood in a very general way can be much more liberal than a strong mathematical concept. The riddle analogy was not offered by chance. Any usual method of *clustering* can be applied; the *Nearest Neighbor* method can be preferred for easy updating. Three preferences in the choice of computing methods should be considered: first, updating by new data, second, updating by changing the metric, third — if possible — a charactistic visualization. The goal of the game is the usual clustering one: finding surfaces for efficient discrimination (or finding a metric for that process) and looking for a minimal dimensional representation, i.e. filtering the irrelevant and extracting the decisive factors. (This suggests the application of factor analysis methods.) This experimentation period is not only a part of preliminary efforts but should be a basic ingredient of the system to be used, i.e. the user should receive an easily manageable system that allows further checks of hypotheses, new viewpoints, reorganization of the patterns, review of the metric, inclusion of new items, etc. As expert systems develop towards knowledge services provided by networks, user groups should contribute to achieving these continuous improvement goals, controlled by some conventions on codification procedures, warrants, and warnings. The estimations of a smaller group can hardly be reliable, due to the intrinsic uncertainty of the problem statement, hence a better statistic can be based only on a wide range of experience and by paying special attention to common definitions. Considering this very important latter remark, all possible means of demonstration and clarification should be added to the system as a possibly undetachable, intrinsic ingredient. The medical expert system we have experience with includes a videotape demonstration of each pattern that can be defined or illustrated in a visual way. Let us suppose that we obtained a collection of necessary patterns, such as chapters of a textbook. The next step should be the design of the dynamic: creating the means for thinking in analogies, putting the new patterns into the framework of the existing prototypes. The clustering step can be, if it is really satisfactory, a first aid for estimating the dynamic; if a good, discriminating metric exists, the problem can be solved by adjusting the new pattern to the fixed scale (or scales).

Multidimensional scaling, especially for these purposes, has been developed in the past decades in cognitive psychology, just for bidirectional usage: clustering toward conceptual entities or visualization, recognition, i.e. unification and in the other direction: discrimination. A nice example of these achievements is *Chernoff*'s application for recognition of different human faces. This is based on the fact that in our evolutionary development we had to improve our facial recognition abilities the most.

Unfortunately this is not enough in several cases. As we have emphasized before, the pattern is a multivariate set. While a reduction can be helpful under certain circumstances, the reduction to a scalar distance is *per se* an extreme loss of information. This can reflect a certain momentary view, but all critical investigations and reviews which could be influenced by the simplification are excluded. The statement is true even in the cases where we incorporate several weighed items into the distance measure as well. It is a coding which cannot be reversed.

5.10 Using hierarchy and analogies

 Further lessons of pattern recognition can be helpful. In visual pattern recognition, people and procedures usually discriminate among different levels of vision, i.e. low level vision is identified with edge detection or similar elementary operations, a possible parallel to linear metric. The higher levels take an analog of the human vision system, a hierarchical composition of patterns from picture elements to cognition of the objects, scenarios, etc. The process is not a straightforward one; stored images and other information operate in a closed loop with the different vision functions, anticipation of the picture accelerates, enhances, and frequently deceives cognition. Pattern recognition for encounters with more complex images applies similar methods, anticipates using knowledge bases, builds higher complexity patterns from lower ones, and composes several different kinds of visual information, e.g. shadings, textures, colors, perspectives, etc. The evaluation of this parallel and hierarchical information is organized by a conceptual model; the edge, the texture, etc. are composed in their symbolic representation, in a direct or indirect manner by the usual linguistic labels (e.g. sharp edge, red cube, high tree, two-storied house).

Pipelining in computer architecture applies a simplistic anticipatory model of this type of processing.

The patterns of any intelligent system are similar, they are conceptual compositions of how the physician puts together the patterns of different organs and functions, how the judge develops the whole case from the social environment, the opinion of the Forensic Medical Institute, exhibits, etc.

Our problem now is how to apply these combinations of pattern elements and subpatterns.

One direction can be the further study of human analogical thinking, the ways humans find similarities or make associations. The final objective of this pattern thinking is just this similarity-associativity mechanism. Some typical analogs are:

- *structural* — e.g. the tree structure of genealogy, data hierarchy, etc.;
- *morphological* — typical examples in cells, chromosomes, radiology pictures, shapes of objects, characteristic defects, etc.;
- *instancing* — containing the same item or something of the same group (one typical way is "that corner reminds me of Joe, we met here");
- *coexistential* — the other way of remembering or associating: grouping two or more items by a common type, or, on the contrary, noting an item as a strange occurrence (a church and a cleric — snow and palmtree);
- *dynamic* — a pattern of change (or a complement of change, i.e. stability while others change) mostly related to static pattern analogs (bird — aeroplane).

This classification (which is neither exhaustive nor unique by far) can be used in two ways. One is to search for such kinds of pattern types and to look for a metric in the new space, i.e. in the space of these selected analogies. If the search can be mechanized, these types are very near to an algorithmic classification scheme. (For example, instancing is a rather simple data processing task, as is a search for coexistence.) These schemes were well applied in our medical expert system, where the dynamic features played a special role. The system concerned is related to the introduction of new experimental methods in neonatology, i.e. to fast changes in a great number and variety of phenomena (e.g. brain dimensions, sensory reactions, motion patterns, mental development, etc.). A very simple example of structural relationships is the deviation-inheritance pattern of a family.

The history of discoveries records many structure-related patterns, such as the analogies of atomic structures to the planetary system, analogical thinking in chemical structures, the double helix of molecular biology and its staircase analog, etc. The other direction of application for these kinds of analogies is the representation for man-machine methodologies such as visualization. We shall come back to this point later.

The modest practical results and the infinite range of the general problem is confirmed by the analogy exercises. To illustrate this difficulty, a quotation from *Putnam*: "When Carnap and I worked together on inductive logic in 1953-54, the problem that he regarded as the *most* intractable in the whole area of inductive logic was the problem of giving proper weight to analogy! No criterion is known for distinguishing '*good*' from '*bad*' analogies."

5.11 Pattern—relativity

We now have a feeling for how pattern representation can be combined with the linguistic one and the latter with a semantic analysis of situations and the task of setting an appropriate agenda. A
sophisticated system can have many loops: a visual pattern (or visual-analog pattern) of linguistic data and a linguistic interpretation of the pattern as a basis for logical reasoning. The human mind does it perma-nently, as we mentioned in speaking about prototype and conceptual-symbolic representations and their regular cross-reactions.

The relativity of patterns should be underlined. This is an essential feature of the concept and very important compared to other expert sys-tem methods. The same pattern can have very different meanings for different persons, in different situations, at different times. Very simple symbols, such as the swastika, can have the same feature. It was one of the most ancient, archaic symbols used since the upper paleolithic peri-od. In ancient India, the meaning was related to good and represented light and generosity—now it is the symbol of genocide and extreme hatred.

The discriminating feature can be found either within the pattern, or beyond it in a very volatile context, and this is the more frequent and interesting case. The same situation can be distressing or attracting, tranquilizing or disturbing for different people involved in the case and this is not only a subjective reaction. In complex technological processes the same phenomenon can be a signal of a dangerous disturbance or the success of a critical high-yield procedure. A similar feature is character-ized in some expert systems and shells by viewpoints and focusing. All previous issues can be reviewed from this aspect, i.e. a special focus realized by changing weights, distance definitions, by further modification of structural or morphological templates, emphasis on special features, data, etc. The solution as given by this narrative looks to be simple — but any such view is a misleading interpretation. The focus can be predetermined, as are certain objectives of medical diagnosis, but the focus itself can be the object of investigation. Any different viewpoint has a pointer to previous considerations of logic; this is the problem of multiple worlds (*Kripke*), situational-dialog logic. The obvious fact is that each viewpoint focusing technique increases the complexity of the system, with a danger of combinatorial explosion. A pragmatic approach is extremely important but a broad view of possibilities, a wide background of experimentation during development, is an important requirement as well, since a human expert generally has a considerably broader background knowledge than is required for the task in a narrow sense. The situation between the development of an expert system and the user-level application is similar.

Phylogeny developed a special switching mechanism for values and viewpoints: the change of emotional status [Oatley 1989]. Love, hunger, a feeling of danger, a drive for dominance, all can change focus very fast and — returning to our paradigm of chess — psychologists now have a lot of experience about how these emotional switches influence the beautiful game of logic. The *Polgár* girls of Section 5.6 were mostly trained to play against men, because male and female styles are different, the female style is less aggressive, and this must be the reason for the apparent minority of women in chess.

5.12 Cognition as a projection of lower dimensions

The Descartes-Turing-test problem recurs from age to age. The earlier versions aimed more at emphasizing the superiority of the human, his divine substance; the later versions aimed more at understanding mechanisms of the mind. But because of the very nature of the problem, they always mixed the two goals, to some extent. The latest relevant contributions were *Putnam*'s [1981] metaphor of isolated *brains in a vat* with sensory inputs, and *Searle*'s [1980, 1990] idea of the *Chinese room* where an innocent person assigns input Chinese characters to different Chinese characters as output by certain fixed rules of assignment. The person who does the task, otherwise completely detached from the environment, knows nothing about the meaning of the Chinese ideograms, he acts like a program, manipulating symbols by certain rules. Putnam's brain in the vat has some similar features, all sorts of inputs and outputs, but lacking the human experience of the continuous contextual and emotional environment of the body. The main issue is the complexity and profundity of the concept *understanding*. One trivial answer at present is a comparison of the complexity. The brain has about 10^{11} neurons and each of those has about 10^3 synaptic connections. The brain must be even more complex because of brain dynamics and other nontrivial neural functions and activities.

There are two further unclear issues, expressed in our computer science paradigms as *memory organization* and *inference engine*. These are the focus of research from all sides by related disciplines. The physical existence of some pattern primitives, e.g. shape and color, is well-demonstrated by *Poggio* [1973], *Julesz* [1981], *Marr* [1985], and several others, as is a higher dynamic organization demonstrated by *Hubel* and *Wiesel* [1979], and others. The physical-biological process of rotating an object in the mind was proved, the time required to process the fact is nearly proportional to the angle of rotation. Here we find a later version of basic concepts resident in our mind either as a result of evolution or by socialization and training, but prewired in any case. This is somehow a return in reverse of the Platonic idea, but the mirror of the mind is a mirror of the phylogenetic and ontogenetic evolutionary experience.

The situation with the *inference engine* is similar. The mind reflects the relations with a teleological aspect and in many cases it has worked wonderfully! The least effort principle of *Fermat-Huyghens-D'Alembert-Hamilton* is an excellent example of that; other similar principles include the set of conservation laws (energy, impulse, etc.), or the notion of symmetry. The notion of *horror vacui* (Nature abhors a vacuum) worked only for a short time in gas dynamics.

Human perception was always teleological. It stored and organized everything according to our interests: Survival and all other delicate and less delicate interest branchings of survival, even esthetics or ethics, belong here as well. This interest-ordered organization of experience works because it is a kind of mirror of the natural organization perceived in Nature, a strong meta-phor: *one* viewpoint of Reality's patterns. Another level of the reverse-Platonic!

Using our mirror viewpoint metaphor further: A projection into a lower dimension, with a certain scale, is a workable representation up to a certain limit. We reach this limit when the view from another projection does not provide contradictory evidence. Here we reach the equivalence and refutation criteria for opposite approaches, objective vs. subjective, causal vs. evidential, and teleological vs. spontaneous. At the same time we met another — also ancient — relevance of logic: to discover the limitations of these singular projections, that is, to help search for viewpoints in higher dimensions, the anatomy of hypercomplexity. Science does it, with some success, but never knows the real cardinality of Nature's dimensions. We return to the God's-eye concept: a view of infinite dimensions without reduction to any further projection.

5.13 Last words: neural computer? — Man-machine!

Most details of these methodologies and metaphoric reasoning can be captured within the framework of conventional computer hardware and software methods. The computer power required to cope with the combinatorial explosion problem, of course, goes beyond this statement. Nevertheless some new configurations may have beneficial features. Neural computation* is especially oriented to pattern matching. It should not be forgotten that neural nets cannot operate anything more than the usual equipment, but comparison of patterns can be executed in a more flexible, faster, more parallel way. The basic algorithm for matching the contents of the neural cells can be adjusted to reflect the choice of dimensions. The quadratic formulae of energy-type neural algorithms are ideal parallels to distance measures. The matrix organization of a neural scheme is extremely suitable for the comparison of patterns where the metric, in most cases, can be represented by vectors. These remarks indicate that neural schemes combined with conventional computers and probably specially organized storage can advance our goals in an optimal way — for the time being and for the near future.

---

* [Smolensky 1988; Sompolinsky 1988; Hopfield 1985; Valiant 1985; Hillis 1987]

Connectionist models of brain and parallel computation support these pattern-based aspects. Not only can we quote the advanced results concerning the visual cortex's activity or neural nets' lessons, but also further developments of *Hofstadter*'s ants' paradigm. The ants' neural system contains about 10^5 times less components than the human brain, but they are organized in societies which have just about the same component magnitude in population. This does not mean that an ant society can compete with a human brain, but, as a system connected by information, they can develop several collective responses which are much beyond the capabilities of the individual ant and achieve a high-level coordination based on simple, rule-like interactions. The ants' society develops different and appropriate patterns (in our sense) without a conceptual hierarchy. *Prima facie,* a further development of this idea for everyone who looks at these phenomena, is an optimistic view of mankind as contributing to the human superbrain composed of information networks and assisted by computational vehicles! We can attribute something like an advent to this idea of the adoption of new, global values and principles, e.g. human rights or ecological priorities.

This lesson is probably similar to the previous ones. Neural nets are fine practical devices and will be still more useful if large nets, with all their surface and hidden intermediate layers, become available; interconnections of digital or analog processing elements will be perfected on single chips. Nevertheless, as we emphasize, they do not do anything which is theoretically new; the connectionist idea was originated by *von Neumann* himself, the *Hebb* law comes from the late forties, the basic matching algorithms, either deterministic (the least square approximations) or statistical (*Boltzmann* machine), are the classical old workhorses. All these provide a much smaller and much less adaptive, dynamic complexity than the human brain does, according to our recent knowledge.

This means that a further step can be taken towards the infinite limitations of computability, but no major breakthrough can be proved despite this.

No final word, as is sometimes claimed, but a new instrument for more appropriate man-machine systems. This picture of the future as a projection of present trends is only a belief—a humanistic belief, but such is one of the major thrusts of this essay.

Conclusion

A gentle admonition

The reader can be embarrassed by finding an apparent eclecticism of practical and philosophical issues. This was what I could do – because of my background – and what I had to do, because of my convictions. An undertaking such as this essay is always a kind of *Entwicklungsroman* (a novel of personal development). The need for a combination of holistic views with practical ones is a real, practical experience. I suppose I should provide some arguments for that.

I returned a few times to my standpoint on rationalism. We can follow a recent fashion of denial, a belittling of the results of the Age of Reason, an accusation that several of mankind's troubles are due to this belief in Reason. I followed the problems of simplistic rationalisms which had an unconfessed revival in an even more primitive form in several claims of computer science and artificial intelligence. This argumentation does not speak against those wonderful achievements of rational thinking or the foundations of modern science which still govern our present technology. As I mentioned, they were real *Jacob*'s fighting with God himself. This was part of the eternal struggle of the human mind to conquer a part of Reality or allow it to be understood and used in a human rationale: reckoning what and to what extent it has been achieved, and what at present looks to be beyond our mind's capacity. This account helps more to further the progress of the Rational than an irrational belief in a deceptive simplicity. I think that *this* is the rational view.

The contradictions discovered by cognitive psychology about the weaknesses of human judgements, and all investigations concerning the fragility of uncertainty estimates and relativity of logic lead us to an obvious conclusion: the future of decision systems is a flexible, non-dogmatic combination of all available resources. This is the suggestion to use interacting, self-explaining man-machine systems. The best advice that can be given is a plea, or hope, for human education in understanding the pros and cons in one's own mind, in other people's minds, in computer programs, or in logico-mathematical procedures. This understanding can only be well-founded by including the study of epistemology and its entire process of evolution throughout our cultural history. It involves the development of a sensitive feeling for looking deeper, looking from different directions, and thinking in the mysterious metric of time, as well as a sensitivity for continuity and change as parallel processes. Science and art are the expressions, documents, demonstrations of this process, which is eternal in the human conceptual framework. *Therefore, for a quickly expanding intelligent machine environment, we need more and more education in this historical-traditional sense of culture.* Maybe this is the ultimate lesson of this essay.

Logic programming is looking for fixed points, transformations that preserve some relationships in the original meaning but change the context for a new goal. *Felix Klein* [1872] suggested searching for invariances in the definition of mathematical disciplines. We hope that these fixed points have been well emphasized in this essay: a *"critique of practical reason"* (the expression is pilfered from *Kant*!), i.e. an estimation of practical results, usefulness of methods, a view of looking for invariances in the historical ways of human thinking, and of the deeper reasons of this invariance, and last, keeping one's eyes open for new intellectual and practical challenges, putting them into new frameworks when it is promising and useful but not being dazzled by fashionable shibboleths.

What have we probably accomplished and what did we not? We hope that we could provide a somewhat different and useful view of epistemological problems related to evolving computer-assisted and interlocked human activities. Returning to the preface, I use here the first person plural intentionally because I assumed those cooperative readers who helped me in clarifying my views—thank you! Maybe you have appreciated this sometimes unusual and seemingly confused usage of the first singular and plural. I hope that the introductory explanation was somehow justified.

Let us recapitulate these notions in short theses:

1. Any final result in imitating the human mind, or even further, finding of a general problem solver and thereby creating an omnipotent God-machine or Evil, is beyond our considerations. We take the admonition of *Putnam* in earnest: "try not to imitate the human mind but write clever programs". (Nevertheless, the interpretation of the word *'clever'* was the subject of this book—with limited success.) Several problems related to excessive complexity and an inherent infinity of possible cases are unsolvable, according to our present scientific conviction. Nevertheless, computer science and those efforts which have accompanied the entire progress of human thinking could and can be more helpful than is generally supposed, if used in an appropriate way.

2. The first statement has several consequences. We should look at problems and their solution methods in the same analytic and synthetic way we generally use these methods themselves. This means that *no perfect method or final solution exists*; each methodology, uncertainty handling, logic, linguistic means, or patterns should be applied in an orchestrated way, and the se-

lection of methods or approaches within one of these larger conceptual-methodological directions is not a matter of religious belief in one method or the other but a pragmatic, *ad hoc* choice based first on the nature of the problem and also on computational requirements, achievable objectives, software environments, experience, etc.

3. Thus, a *continuous critical analysis* is needed in every problem solving task, before and after the work is done.

4. The *orchestrating* of the methods can be improved if it is done not only from the point of view of the most up-to-date state of the art. It is better understood and put in the right place if a wide-angle, horizontal and vertical point of view can be used. Horizontal here means using insights behind the method's mathematical, algorithmic properties to related knowledge of the models themselves, i.e. physical, physiological, psychological, etc. analysis of what the pros and cons, the limits and freedoms of the model applied are. Vertical here means a historico-philosophical perspective: how are the ideas leading to the present model developed, what are really new aspects and why, what is only reinvented and renamed? This perspective is not a snobbish cultural beauty-mark but actively helps the critical aspect, the selection of methods, the avoidance of superficial, fashion-driven, intellectual uniforms. It helps in getting to that kind of wide-angled but analytical ability mentioned above.

5. According to *Donald Knuth*, programming is more an art than a technique (nevertheless not only the ancient Greeks considered these two as not really separated). This is even more valid for a much higher intellectual activity, in the design of in-

telligent systems. The word *'orchestrating'* was not chosen by chance. This requires fine analytical work in details, a broad, holistic, synthetic view of the entire problem, and a deep discernment of an extensive environment. It should develop as a high art of the present and future, with a high responsibility for mankind.

If we agree on those — OK!

and/or

Appendices

1 Probabilistic logic

It is a *monotonic* approach to reasoning in the presence of uncertainty proposed by N.J. Nilsson in 1986. In a precise technical sense, truth values of sentences of a formal system are replaced by probabilities.

Let $S = \{S_1, S_2, \ldots S_n\}$ be a finite set of sentences of a logical system (such as first order logic). In a model of our formal system some of the S_i must be true and the others must be false. Let $W_1, W_2, \ldots W_m$ be the consistent (i.e. simultaneously satisfiable) sets of formulas of the form $\{F_1, F_2, \ldots F_n\}$ where F_j is either S_j or $\neg S_j$.

Clearly we have $m \leq 2^n$. The sets W_i are called *worlds*. Such a world (W_1) would be the set: $S_1 =$ Joe is tall (true); $S_2 =$ Mary is small (true); $S_3 =$ Mary likes boys who are smaller than her (false). In another world (W_2) the relations would be different. Motivated by the fact, that the actual world is exactly one of the W_i, Nilsson considers the sample space whose atoms are $W_1, W_2, \ldots W_m$. If P is a probability measure on this space, then, using event algebra, we infer the following relations:

(PL) $$P(S_j) = \sum_{S_j \in W_i} P(W_i), \quad j = 1, \ldots n.$$

The central algorithmic problem in this theoretical framework is the *probabilistic entailment problem*. Perhaps the most important special case is the following: suppose that we have the values (beliefs) $\pi_i = P(S_i)$ for $i = 1, \ldots n - 1$. Our aim is to obtain information on the possibility of the last sentence, or putting it another way, on the possible values of $P(S_n)$. This means that the different worlds have different probabilities. If they were certain, then an apparent contradiction would arise among the sentences of the different worlds.

The equations (PL) together with the restrictions expressing that P is a probability measure, (i.e. $0 \leq P(W_i) \leq 1$ and $\sum P(W_i) = 1$) give a system of linear inequalities. Such systems can be handled by methods from convex geometry and linear programming. In particular, it is known that the feasible values of $P(S_n)$ (the ones compatible with our initial beliefs) constitute a (possibly empty) closed interval.

As an example we look at the following simple set of three sentences $S = \{p, q, p \supset q\}$ where p and q can assume both truth values independently. In this case we readily obtain that $m = 4$ and we can put

$$W_1 = \{p, q, p \supset q\}, \quad W_2 = \{\neg p, q, p \supset q\},$$

$$W_3 = \{\neg p, \neg q, p \supset q\}, \quad W_4 = \{p, \neg q, \neg(p \supset q)\}.$$

Assume now that we have the initial beliefs $\pi_1 = \pi_2 = 0.5$. The relations (PL) yield

$$0.5 = P(W_1) + P(W_4)$$

$$0.5 = P(W_1) + P(W_2)$$

$$0.5 = P(W_1) + P(W_2) + P(W_3).$$

The last two equations and $P(W_3) \geq 0$ imply that $\pi_3 \geq 0.5$. The distribution P^* defined by $P^*(W_1) = P^*(W_3) = 0.5$ and $P^*(W_2) = P^*(W_4) = 0$ is clearly compatible with the constraints at hand and gives $P^*(p \supset q) = 1$. Similarly $\pi_3 = 0.5$ can also be attained as shown by the distribution P' given by $P'(W_1) = P'(W_3) = 0$ and $P'(W_2) = P(W_4) = 0.5$. As a conclusion, the possibilities for π_3 can be summarized in the inequalities $0.5 \leq \pi_3 \leq 1$.

For n large the computations required to solve the probabilistic entailment problem are apparently impractical. Nilsson considers approximation schemes to partially circumvent this difficulty.

As *Pearl* [1988] points out: "The way probabilistic logic deals with partially specified models is opposite to the way the *D-S theory* does it." (See D-S in Appendix 3.) "Both methods accept specifications in the form of logical sentences and allow a probability assignment to a subset of these sentences. However, whereas probabilistic logic treats probabilistic models as object-level theories and treats logical relations as meta-constraints on such theories, the D-S theory reverses these roles: Logical constraints serve as object-level theory, within which deductions take place, and probabilistic information is treated as meta-constraints that modify (randomly) these theories. The two systems represent two ways of viewing the mixture of soft (probabilistic) and hard (logical) information items in our possession. Probabilistic logic views this mixture as a layer of hard restrictions imposed on a set of soft models, while D-S theory views it as a layer of soft restrictions imposed on a set of hard models.

Since the two paradigms produce different numerical responses to what appears to be the same set of queries, the choice between the two is clearly not arbitrary; it depends on the nature of the problem we wish to solve. When our task is one of synthesis (e.g. the class scheduling problem), the constraints are externally imposed and our concern really centers on issues of possibility and necessity—so the D-S theory offers a better representation for the anticipated queries. However, when we face a task of analysis (e.g. diagnosis, as in the Three Prisoners dilemma) where we are trying to piece together a model of physical reality, the constraints are merely by-products of our ignorance, and the probabilistic approach is more suitable, whether in probabilistic logic or the Bayesian manifestation."

In most cases the set of the (PL) equations is undetermined and then using the *entropy* concept ($H = -P^t \log P$)—where P^t is the transpose of P—and the maximizing methods by Lagrange multipliers, a *maximum entropy* distribution can be obtained for ranking the probabilities [Jaynes 1957]. This seemingly attractive approach results in a high computational complexity and increased uncertainty used for really interesting complex tasks.

2 Bayesian methods

The Bayesian method establishes relations between *a priori* and *a posteriori* probabilities, i.e. between two events which are cause and consequence related and vice versa. If

$p(a)$ is the probability estimate of an event (e.g. people salting their food twice higher than the average), and

$p(b)$ the probability of a certain consequence (e.g. people having a high blood pressure), and

$p(b/a)$ the statistics of people who have high blood pressure among those who are excessively salting, then

$p(a/b)$ is the estimate of looking for a cause b in presence of a (e.g. for supposing a habit of excessive salting in a case of high blood pressure) and this will be

$$(\text{B-1}) \qquad\qquad p(a/b) = \frac{p(b/a)p(a)}{p(b)}$$

If there are many (n) possible reasonings (consequences), the formula for one of them will be modified to

$$(\text{B-2}) \qquad\qquad p(a_1/b) = \frac{p(b/a_1)p(a_1)}{\sum_{j=1}^{n} p(a_j)p(b/a_j)}$$

(in our example high blood pressure caused by salting, neurosis, kidney problems, sclerosis, etc.) as a consequence and having a statistics of those singular sets of events. The doctor looks for the cause of the certain symptom, ranking the hypotheses by this formula.

A further extension is updating, i.e. including new data into the existing statistics:

If $b_1, b_2, \ldots b_m$ are different poolings of evidences for b, then

(B-3) $P(a_1|b_1 \& b_2 \& b_3 \ldots \& b_m) = \dfrac{P(b_1 \& b_2 \& b_3 \ldots \& b_m | a_1) P(a_1)}{\sum_{j=1}^{n} p(a_j) P(b_1 \& b_2 \& b_3 \ldots \& b_m)}$

(high blood pressure statistics of m years, n countries, updated year by year, country by country).

The Bayesian method is a strong probabilistic one, i.e. it supposes the independence of events, time invariance, the excluded middle, etc. For AI considerations the most severe condition is the crisp classification of cases (concepts, definitions a and b), i.e. the prejudice included in the statistics or other estimates.

3 Dempster-Shafer method

The method is composed really of two parts: Dempster's rule of combination of evidences and Shafer's application of it for a calculus and philosophy of evidence distribution among certain events and groups of events, events where we have an estimate and those where the chances are completely hidden.

The Dempster rule [1967] for two elements was stated accurately by *Johan Heinrich Lambert* in his *Neues Organon* published in 1764 [Shafer 1976]. Some parts of the problem go back to *Jacob Bernoulli*, early 18th century. The problem is the following: if we have some estimates (beliefs, evidences, chances, poolings) on a set of events and another partly different set, or different combination of estimates for the same situation (in Shafer's wording: the frame of discernment), how should they be combined to get a resulting estimate? Typical examples are sets of different symptoms of one certain malady or sets of different evidences in a criminal case.

Dempster's rule suggests an orthogonal sum of the estimates in the following way:

$A = (A_1 \ldots A_n)$ a set of events (symptoms etc.)

$B = (B_1 \ldots B_n)$ the other set of the same situation

$m_1(A_i)$, $m_2(B_j)$ are the related estimates; each set of those should be complete $(\sum m_i = 1)$,

then for the combination (intersection) $A_i \cap B_j = S$

(D-S-1)
$$m(S) = \frac{\displaystyle\sum_{\substack{ij \\ A_i \cap B_j = S}} m_1(A_i)\, m_2(B_j)}{1 - \displaystyle\sum_{\substack{ij \\ A_i \cap B_j = 0}} m_1(A_i)\, m_2(B_j)} \ .$$

The denominator serves for discarding the empty parts of the ·intersections and for normalization to the measure 1.

It can be seen that this method leads to an unsurmountable number of multiplications in each complex case. All detailed evidences, estimates should have their cross-effects especially if there are several sets of estimates, and not only two. The method can be extended similarly to any other number of those sets; Shafer proved its commutative and associative features. The application of the method can be improved by skillful partitioning, coarsening, but it is basically fast growing in real complex situations. Some contradictions of the Dempster rule are demonstrated by the *Zadeh paradox* (see next page). Shafer put the method into a firm mathematical framework and extended the philosophy of the system for enabling it to manage unknown events and their combinations. In this process he introduced several important concepts.

The first is the *frame of discernment*, i.e. the totality of events and their combinations within a certain situation (case). The strength of this concept is that it manages combined evidences as, e.g. symptoms which can conclude to more than one disease, but its weakness is the mentioned combinatorial feature. The concept of the frame of discernment permits one to define estimates to all known cases and their combinations and leave the remainder to the whole territory of the unknown. By combining the different sets of these estimates (different investigations, different witnesses, etc.) the uncertainty of this unknown region (remainder of the frame of discernment) decreases gradually. This is the effect what we mentioned under smearing the evidences through the possible cases.

One certain case of evidence (one symptom, one statement of a witness) is a *basic probability assignment* (the values in the Dempster method), the *belief function* is the sum of those for a subset of the frame (Bel A)). The *plausibility function* is a complement:

(D-S-2) $$\mathrm{Pl}(A) = 1 - \mathrm{Bel}(A)$$

A detailed but well-digestable presentation of the method is given in the basic book of *Shafer* [1976]. A very good practical demonstration can be found in the MYCIN book [Buchanan and Shortliffe 1984]. A great amount of critical discussions is available, reference can be made here to Chapter 9 of *Pearl's* book [1988], to [Perez 1989a-b] and an extremely interesting discussion with comments and rejoinders [Shafer, Lindley and Spiegelhalter 1987] where the original concept, a more orthodox, and a more pragmatic one are confronted.

Zadeh-paradox — The example demonstrates the inadequacy of the *Dempster* rule for marginal values. With notations of the Appendix on the D-S method

$$m_1(A) = 0.9; \quad m_1(B) = 0.1; \quad m_1(C) = 0.0 \quad \left(\sum m_1 = 1 \right)$$

$$m_2(A) = 0.0; \quad m_2(B) = 0.1; \quad m_2(C) = 0.9 \quad \left(\sum m_2 = 1 \right),$$

apply the rule (D-S-1), we get $m(A) = 0.0; m(B) = 1.0; m(C) = 0.0$ which is a contradictory crisp deterministic result. Although the evidences from the first set of polling (experiments, tests, investigations, etc.) yielded a high value for case A and from the second set for the case B, they hardly can be neglected for a final decision. Shafer suggested some improvements for avoiding these difficulties but several other examples were created to indicate the uncertainty of this and other methods.

4 Certainty Factor procedures

This method was developed for medical consultation systems where subjective estimates have a primary role, statistics are weak and the diagnostic process is not too sensitive to slight differences in numerical guesses. According to the *CF* method, the expert sets a belief of pros between 0 and 1 (values under 0.2 taken as zero) and the cons in the same way. The first is the *measure of belief (MB)*, the second the *measure of disbelief (MD)*.

The Certainty Factor *(CF)*

$$CF' = MB - MD \qquad \text{and standardized:}$$

$$CF = \frac{MB - MD}{1 - \min(MB, MD)}.$$

The combination rule:

$$CF_{\text{comb}}(X, Y) = \begin{cases} X + Y(1 - X) & X, Y > 0 \\ \frac{X+Y}{1 - \min(|X|,|Y|)} & \text{one of } X, Y < 0 \\ -CF_{\text{comb}}(-X, -Y) & X, Y < 0 \end{cases}.$$

The above model is further refined but this short insight is sufficient for reading our text. The MYCIN book [Buchanan and Shortliffe 1984] offers a very clear and readable detailed presentation. It should be mentioned only that the calculation of the increase of beliefs is done analogously to the Bayesian and the final results are not too much different from the D-S method. This feature is emphasized by the authors.

5 Possibility – fuzzy methods

The basic idea of Zadeh is the fact that conceptual frames are not crisp, i.e. the sets defined by people have no well-defined borders. The fuzzy set is not such a crisply defined set and the *membership values* attributed to the set components (events, facts, data, etc.) are representations of the belief, estimation, and contextual dependency of belonging to the set. This means that the fuzzy membership value is consciously context-dependent, and has a semantics. The property of attributing this semantics opens the possibility of a direct use for a linguistic interface and for the development of a fuzzy language. The distribution concept of the probability theory has a simplified version by a trapezoid distribution, where the lower and the upper limits of the enclosed area are the *possibility* (resp. *necessity*) limits of the set definition. Combination is somehow relative to the same theoretic solutions and this is not by chance: the problem is for both to get a reliable estimate of uncertain events' coincidence.

In the fuzzy notation $\mu_F(F)$ is the membership function of a set F, i.e. μ_{iF} expresses how the element i is guessed to be belonging to the set F. $\sum \mu_i(F) = 1$ as in any similar uncertainty methods. The membership guess can be expressed by words, e.g. high, low, very cold, hot, etc. Both possibilistic and fuzzy logic are built upon this concept.

Possibilistic logic is concerned with uncertain reasoning where the database is a fuzzy description of a given world.

The fuzzy combination rules:

union: $\mu_\cup = \max \mu_i$

intersection: $\mu_\cap = \min \mu_i$

for possibility extimation $\pi(u)$ are defined, the degree of possibility that the datum concerned (the height of Mary or the temperature next day at noon) is exactly equal to u by this definition; two further values can be conceptualized, an upper bound named possibility (Π) and a lower bound, the necessity (N)

$$\Pi = \sup_u \min(\mu(u), \ \pi(u))$$

$$N = \inf_u \max(\mu(u), \ 1 - \pi(u)).$$

Based on these concepts a complete logic is established with the fuzzy-possibilistic analogs of quantifiers and syllogisms [Zadeh 1965, 1989; Dubois and Prade 1988].

6 Endorsement

Endorsement is an attempt to avoid any uncertainty calculus—that is the reason why it was specially mentioned in the book. The paradigm of the method demonstrated by the SOLOMON program is modelling portfolio investment. It tries to simulate the human decision maker who classifies some possible future actions and logs pros and cons which support or disagree with one or the other action. This activity is not a weighted classification but the rules are collected by the specific experience of the domain expert. In this way the method uses logic as vehicle but its real appearance is nearer to the pattern situation view. The system contains the tasks and the endorsement background, e.g. domain inference rules, rules for task scheduling, propagation of endorsements over inferences. The endorsement types are similar to the fuzzy attributes: *exact, necessary, flexible, inflexible* and related to the subject: *corroborating, conflicting, redundant,* etc. The procedure is finally controlled by the programmed specific evaluations of the domain expert, i.e. it is—in this orthodox form, not combined with any other method—a recipe for one very specific subject in a strictly closed world.

7 Lambda calculus

The λ-operator is a variable binder in the modal predicate logic.

$\lambda x S$ denotes the sentence: x variable is a member of set S (e.g. $\lambda x G$ can be interpreted as x (Mary, Ann, Margaret, Bess) are girls but in a later context should be defined as the one who next plays the role of Juliet. In that way this is a kind of abstraction (λ abstraction) as well. The list of variables (the girls enumerated) are the formal parameters of the λ expression.

8 Nonmonotonic logic

In a system of an open world not all statements corroborate the previous ones, or those hypotheses or conclusions which are logical antecedents or consequences of these statements. Monotonic logic is created in a closed world where all further statements, data and facts add to the validity of the previous ones.

Nonmonotonic logic looks at these contradictory sets of statements and attempts to find a consistent way of resolving the situation by adding further new conditions or canceling some old ones.

In classical logic all theorems are results of valid inferences, in nonmonotonic logic one starts with all inferred statements, whether they are consistent or not. Then in most cases one starts to find a fixed point, i.e. a minimal set where all statements get a consistent context. A typical paradigm is *Tweety* the bird (see App 14, Sec. 3.4, 3.6).

Several methods were developed for restoring consistency, e.g. circumscription, default, autoepistemic logic, partly the Truth Maintenance Systems.

9 Circumscription

"We know some objects in a given class and we have some ways of generating more. We jump to the conclusion that this gives all the objects in the class. Thus we *circumscribe* the class to the objects we know how to generate."

"It is only a conjecture, because there might be an object such that" a predicate on the object "is not generated in this way." "The heuristics of circumscription—when one can plausibly conjecture that the objects generated in known ways are all there are—are completely unstudied.

Circumscription is not deduction in disguise, because every form of deduction has two properties that circumscription lacks—transitivity and what we may call monotonicity. Transitivity says that "if a is a consequence of b and c is a consequence of b, then c is a consequence of a. (If snowing, the road is slippery, if slippery then driving is dangerous, consequently if snowing then driving is dangerous.) In realistic cases (circumscription) driving on snow by a car equipped with tire chains is not dangerous. Monotonicity says that within a class of statements all further sentences corroborate the statement further. No exception or contradiction occurs. This is not the case in circumscription and generally in *nonmonotonic logic* because we find some exceptional cases, e.g. our penguin Tweety is a bird which does not fly. The way of circumventing this difficulty is to find a minimum model where all sentences are true (e.g. European birds, cars with standard, low mileage tires, etc.). Nevertheless "It is not always true that a sentence true in all minimal models can be proved by circumscription. Indeed, the minimal model of Peano's axiom is the standard model of arithmetic and Gödel's theorem is the assertion that not all true sentences are theorems. Minimal models don't always exist, and when they exist, they are not always unique."*

10 Default logic

This is a method [Reiter 1980] for treating nonmonotonic problems. The basic idea is a distinction between general "hard" rules (facts) and their defaults, i.e. those rules which extend the world of the fact by exemptions and irregularities. (All birds fly but penguins do not.) The method is similar to circumscription, the main difference is the theoretically well-formed idea of circumscription's minimal set, related to the fixed point theorems. A weakness of default logic is the arbitrary and occasional nature of the default rules. They cannot be inferred within the system, they can be used for further inference with much caution, and they can yield trivial contradictions.

---

*The quotations are from *McCarthy* [1977], the logical formulae are substituted by verbal explanation and examples.

11 Autoepistemic logic

Autoepistemic logic [Stalnaker 1980, Moore 1985] is a typical conceptual frame of a closed world. It contains a set of beliefs of an agent and a language which can generate this kind of a closed world. The hierarchical version takes a set of those which can interact but they are closed in the set of these individual subsets.

In spite of its closeness requirement this logic is nonmonotonic as well, the language can generate nonsense or contradictions from a valid set of beliefs—there is no protection for machines, neither for people!

12 Counterfactuals

This is a logic based on negative, excluding statements. For example, if it would not be a brain injury, it would be an Alzheimer disease. The logical implications are therefore different from regular syllogisms, nevertheless, several of the Aristotelean schemes fully cover the concept, even more it is (was!) extended for possibilistic modalities as well. It is related to nonmonotonic logic and naturally to the different worlds concept [Ginsberg 1986].

13 Truth Maintenance Systems (TMS)

The original idea of Doyle [1979] was an establishment of a bridge between monotonic and nonmonotonic cases. In a monotonic case we have an antecedent precondition, e.g. "It is raining" and logical consequence "we get wet". TMS adds *assumptions* to this ("if we do not take umbrella", "if we go out early", "if we cannot walk under the arcade" etc.). The program maintains the knowledge base of the reasoner. The system checks the truth of the precondition-consequence relations but it does the same for the assumptions, especially if the logical procedure starts to be nonmonotonic (we get wet $\longrightarrow$ get a cold $\longrightarrow$ miss the performance). The TMS revises the assumptions to restore the consistency and informs the reasoner about the process. The relation with the D-S method is just the consideration of a group of conditions, the difference between them may occur, if certain evidences are (or can be) added to these groups and the situations are not simply binary ones.

The ATMS (Assumption-Based Truth Maintenance Systems) [deKleer 1986] is a further development of the same idea, calling the set of assumptions an *environment* and reducing this to a minimal set as it is done by circumscription as well. The closed world assumption is maintained by this procedure and having a conflict the system checks the assumptions until it can return to the monotonic situation.

14 Paradoxes

These were usual logical games for finding contradictions and extending logic by the ancient Greek philosophers, especially by Stoics. Their sophistication opened several relevant channels of thinking. These very useful exercises were similar to those that are used now in nonmonotonic logic, special intensional logic, and different worlds. We quote four celebrated paradoxes of Eubulides [Kneale and Kneale 1971], The Liar, The Hooded, The Bold or The Heap and the Horned, and the Russel paradox (Section 3.5), the Three Prisoners Paradox (Section 2.6) and the Ace of Spades Paradox (Section 3.6), Tweety the penguin-like bird figure (Sec. 3.4, 3.6); some others mentioned in the text: the Nixon diamond, the Yale Shooting problem.

The Nixon diamond — a usual paradigm of nonmonotonic logic. Republicans are mostly non-pacifist, quakers are mostly pacifist. Nixon is simultaneously a quaker and a Republican. The consequence is contradictory, if we do not permit exceptions in the flow of logic or some probabilistic distribution of the two different consequences. The problem is illustrated by a diamond shape:

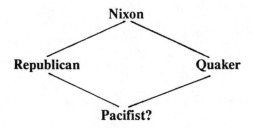

The Yale Shooting Problem — A gun is loaded at a given time and the gun is fired (at Fred) at another time. How can we conclude that Fred is killed or alive? The problem is dependent on the temporal processes—what is the sequence of events? Is the gun in-between somehow unloaded or not?—i.e. on the persistence of situations. The *YSP* is a paradigm for temporal logic, temporal projections [Hanks and McDermott 1986]. (Nevertheless, *Goethe:* "Reduction of the effect to the cause is only a historical procedure, e.g. the effect of a man killed to the cause of the gun fired.")

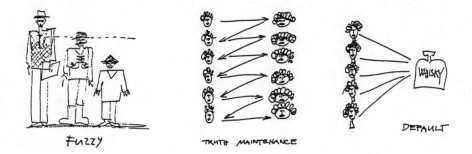

Recommended readings

Boden, M.: Artificial Intelligence and Natural Man, 2nd ed., expanded, MIT Press, Cambridge, Mass., 1987

Brachman, R. J., Levesque, H. J. (eds.): Readings in Knowledge Representation, Morgan Kaufmann, San Mateo, CA, 1985

Collins, A., Smith, E. E. (eds.): Readings in Cognitive Science, a Perspective from Psychology and Artificial Intelligence, Morgan Kaufmann, San Mateo, CA, 1988

Copi, I. M., Gould, J. A. (eds.): Contemporary Readings in Logical Theory, MacMillan, New York, 1972

Dreyfus, H. L., Dreyfus, S.: Mind over Machine, Free Press, New York, 1987

Fodor, J. A.: Modularity of Mind, a Bradford Book, MIT Press, Cambridge, Mass., 1983

Ginsberg, M. L. (ed.): Readings in Nonmonotonic Reasoning, Morgan Kaufmann, San Mateo, CA, 1987

Kneale, W. and M.: The Development of Logic, Oxford University Press, Oxford, 1962

Minsky, M. L.: The Society Theory of Mind, Simon and Schuster, New York, 1986

Oldroyd, D.: The Arch of Knowledge, An Introductory Study of the History of the Philosophy and Methodology of Science, Methuen and Co., London, 1986.

Pearl, J.: Probabilistic Reasoning in Intelligent Systems: Networks of Plausible Inference, Morgan Kaufmann, San Mateo, CA, 1988

Pylyshyn, Z. W.: Computation and Cognition, Toward a Foundation for Cognitive Science, a Bradford Book, MIT Press, Cambridge, Mass., 1984

Tversky, A., Slovic, P., Kahneman, D.: Judgement under Uncertainty: Heuristics and Biases, Cambridge University Press, Cambridge, 1982

Bibliography

Abbreviations

AAAI	American Association for Artificial Intelligence
ACM	Association for Computing Machinery
AI	Artificial Intelligence
IEEE Trans. on PAMI	IEEE Transactions on Pattern Analysis and Machine Intelligence
IEEE Trans. on SMC	IEEE Transactions on Systems, Man and Cybernetics
IJCAI	International Joint Conference on Artificial Intelligence
Proc. IEEE	Proceedings of the Institute of Electrical and Electronics Engineers
Proc. IFAC/SOCOCO	Proceedings of the International Federation of Automatic Control/Software for Computer Control
Proc. Amer. Assoc. Artif. Int.	Proceedings of the American Association for Artificial Intelligence

Abelson, R. P. 1973. The structure of belief systems. In *Computer Models of Thought and Language*, ed. R. C. Schank and K. M. Colby, 287-340. San Francisco: Freeman.

Abelson, R. P. 1981. The psychological status of the script concept. *American Psychologist* 36:715-729

Aiello, L., Cecchi, C., Sartini, D. 1986. Representation and use of meta-knowledge. *Proceedings of the IEEE* 74 (no.10):1304-1321

Allport, D. A. 1980. Patterns and actions, cognitive mechanisms are content specific. In *Cognitive Psychology: New Directions*, ed. G. Claxton, 26-64. London: Routledge and Kegan Paul.

Amarel, S. 1968. On representations of problems of reasoning about actions. In *Machine Intelligence*, vol. 3., 131-172. Edinburgh: Edinburgh University Press.

Amsterdam, J. 1988. Some philosophical problems with formal learning theory. *Proc. AAAI'88*, Saint Paul, Minn., vol. 1-2., 580-584. San Mateo, CA: Morgan Kaufmann.

Arbib, M. A. 1972. *The Metaphorical Brain*. New York: Wiley.

Arbib, M. A. 1981. Perceptual structures and distributed motor control. In *Handbook of Physiology: The Nervous System*, ed. V. B. Brooks, vol. II, 1449-1480. Bethesda, MSD: American Physiological Society.

Arbib, M. A. 1982. Cooperative computation and the cybernetic society. In *Progress in Cybernetics and Systems Research*, ed. R. Trappl, vol. 9., 3-12. Washington: Hemisphere.

Arbib, M. A. and Hanson, A. R. eds., 1988. *Vision, Brain and Cooperative Computation*. Cambridge, Mass.: MIT Press.

Aristotle, 1831. *Aristotelis Opera*—ex recensione Immanuelis Bekkeri (ed. Academia Regia Borussica, MDCCCXXXI—MDCCCLXX, Berlin)

English translations:

The Categories on Interpretation—by Harold P. Cooke

Prior Analytics—by Hugh Tredennick, Cambridge, Mass.: Harvard University Press—London: Heinemann, 1973

Posterior Analytics—by Hugh Tredennick, Cambridge, Mass.: Harvard University Press—London: Heinemann, 1960

The Metaphysics—by E. S. Foster, Cambridge, Mass.: Harvard University Press—London: Heinemann 1955

Topica et Sophistici Elenchi—by W. D. Ross, Oxford: Oxford University Press, 1949

Aristotle, 1912. *Nichomachean Ethics* (Aristotelis Ethica Nicomachea), recognovit Franciscus Suemihl, ed. tertia, Leipzig, Teubner

Babai, L. 1985. Trading group theory for randomness. *Proc. ACM 17th Symposium on Theory of Computer Science*, Providence, R. I., 421-429

Babai, L. 1990. E-mail and the unexpected power of interaction. University of Chicago, Techn. Report CS 90-15

Baker, A., Ginsberg, M. L. 1989. Temporal projection and explanation. *Proc. IJCAI-89*, Detroit, 906-910

Barendregt, H. P. 1984. *The Lambda Calculus: Its Syntax and Semantics*. 2nd ed. Amsterdam: Elsevier.

Barnett, J. A. 1981. Computational methods for a mathematical theory of evidence. *Proc. 7th IJCAI'81*, Vancouver, BC, 868-875

Barwise, J. 1974. *Handbook of Mathematical Logic*. Amsterdam: Elsevier.

Barwise, J., Perry, J. 1983. *Situations and Attitudes*. Cambridge, Mass.: MIT Press.

Bechtel, W. 1988. *Philosophy of mind: an overview for cognitive science*. Hillsdale: Erlbaum.

Berenstein, C., Kanal, L. N., Lavine, D. 1986. Consensus rules. In *Uncertainty in Artificial Intelligence*, ed. L. N. Kanal and J. F. Lemmer, 27-34. Amsterdam: Elsevier.

Bhatnagar, R. K., Kanal, L. N. 1986. Handling uncertain information—a review of numeric and non-numeric methods. In *Uncertainty in*

Artificial Intelligence, ed. L. N. Kanal and J. F. Lemmer, 3-25. Amsterdam: Elsevier.

Bibel, W. 1983. First-order reasoning about knowledge and belief. Draft paper, 13 September 1983

Binford, T. O. 1971. Visual perception by computer. *Proc. IEEE Conference on Systems and Control,* IEEE, Miami, December 1971

Black, M. 1937. Vagueness, an exercise in logical analysis. *Philosophy of Science* 4: 427-455

Blair, D., Pollak, A. R. 1983. Rational collective choice. *Scientific American,* 249 (no. 2):76-83

Boden, M. A., 1981. *Minds and Mechanisms.* Ithaca, NY: Cornell University Press

Boden, M. A., 1987. *Artificial Intelligence and Natural Man.* 2nd ed. London: MIT Press.

Boden, M. A., 1988. *Computer Models of Mind.* Cambridge: Cambridge University Press.

Bonczek, R. H., Holsapple, C. W., Whinston, A. B., 1981. *Foundations of Decision Support Systems.* New York: Academic Press.

Buchanan, B., Shortliffe, E. H., 1984. *Rule-Based Expert Systems, The MYCIN Experiments of the Stanford Heuristic Programming Project.* Reading, Mass.: Addison-Wesley.

Carbonell, J. G., 1982a. Metaphor: an inescapable phenomenon in natural-language comprehension. In *Strategies for Natural Language Processing,* ed. W. G. Lehnert and M. H. Ringle, 415-434. Hillsdale, NJ: Erlbaum.

Carbonell, J. G., 1982b. Experiential learning in analogical problem solving. *Proc. American Association of Artificial Intelligence* 2:168-171

Carnap, R., 1937. *The Logical Syntax of Language*. London: Routledge and Kegan.

Carnap, R., 1947, 1956. *Meaning and Necessity*. Chicago, Ill.: The University Press.

Carnap, R., 1950. *Logical Foundations of Probability*. Chicago, Ill.: University of Chicago Press.

Carnap, R., 1961. *Introduction to Semantics and Formalization of Logic*. Cambridge, Mass.: Harvard University Press.

Carrier, D. H., Wallace, A. W., 1989. An epistemological view of decision-aid technology with emphasis on expert systems. *IEEE Trans. on SMC* 19 (no. 5):1021-1028

Chaitin, G. J., 1987. *Information, Randomness and Incompleteness* — Papers on Algorithmic Information Theory. Singapore: World Scientific.

Cheeseman, P., 1983. A method of computing generalized Bayesian probability values for expert systems. *Proc. IJCAI'83*, Karlsruhe, 198-202

Cheeseman, P., 1985. In defense of probability. *Proc. IJCAI'85*, Los Angeles, 1002-1009

Cheeseman, P., 1986. Probabilistic versus fuzzy reasoning. In *Uncertainty in Artificial Intelligence*, ed. L. N. Kanal and J. F. Lemmer, 85-101. Amsterdam: Elsevier.

Cheeseman, P., Self, M., Kelly, J., Taylor, W., Freeman, D., Stutz, J., 1988. Bayesian classification. *Proc. AAAI'88*, Saint Paul, Minn., vol. 1-2., 607-611. San Mateo, CA: Morgan Kaufmann.

Cheng, Y., Fu, K. S., 1984. Conceptual clustering in knowledge organization. *Proc. 1st Conference on Artificial Intelligence Applications* (sponsored by IEEE Computer Society), Denver, Colo., 274-279

Cherniak, C., 1986. *Minimal Rationality*. Cambridge, Mass.: MIT Press.

Chernoff, H., 1973. The use of faces to represent points in K-dimensional space graphically. *Journal of American Statistical Association* 68:361-368

Chisholm, R. M., 1967. Intentionality. In *The Encyclopedia of Philosophy*, ed. P. Edwards, vol. IV, 201-204. New York: MacMillan.

Chomsky, N., 1957. *Syntactic Structures*. The Hague: Mouton.

Chomsky, N., 1968. *Language and Mind*. New York: Harcourt Brace Jovanovich.

Chomsky, N., 1980. *Rules and Representations*. New York: Columbia University Press.

Chomsky, N., 1984. *Knowledge of Languages: its Nature, Origin and Use*. Cambridge, Mass.: MIT Press.

Church, A., 1936. An unsolvable problem of elementary number theory. *American Journal of Mathematics* 58:345-363.

Church, A., 1941a. *Introduction to Mathematical Logic*. Princeton, NJ: Princeton University Press.

Church, A., 1941b. *The Calculi of Lambda Conversion*. Princeton, NJ: Princeton University Press.

Cliff, N., 1959. Adverbs as multipliers. *Psychological Review* 66 (no. 1):27-44

Clowes, M. B., 1971. On seeing things. *Artificial Intelligence* 2:79-116

Cohen, L. J., 1981. Can human irrationality be experimentally demonstrated? *Behavioral and Brain Sciences* 4:217-345

Cohen, P. R., Loiselle, C. L., 1988. Beyond ISA; structures for plausible inference in semantic networks. *Proc. AAAI'88*, Saint Paul, Minn., 1-2., 415-420. San Mateo, CA: Morgan Kaufmann.

Cohen, P. R., 1985. *Heuristic Reasoning about Uncertainty: An Artificial Intelligence Approach*. Los Altos, CA: Morgan Kaufmann.

Collins, A., Michalski, R. S., 1988. The logic of plausible reasoning: a core theory. *George Mason University, Fairfax, VA, Machine Learning and Inference Lab*, Report, MLI-88-14

Copi, I. M., Gould, J. A., 1964. *Contemporary Readings in Logical Theory*. New York: MacMillan.

Crick, M.C., Marr, D. C., Poggio, T., 1980. *An Information Processing Approach to Understanding the Visual Cortex*. AI Memo, 557. Cambridge, Mass.: MIT Press.

Csányi, V., 1985. How is the brain modelling its environment? A case study by the Paradise Fish. In *Variability and Behavioral Evolution*, ed. G. Montalenti and G. Tecce. *Proc. Accademia Nazionale dei Lincei*, Nr. 259. Roma: Quaderno.

Csányi, V., 1988. Contribution of the genetical and neural memory to animal intelligence. NATO ASI Series, G 17. In *Intelligence and Evolutionary Biology*, ed. H. J. Jerison and I. Jerison, 299-318. Berlin-Heidelberg: Springer.

Csányi, V., 1989. *Evolutionary systems and society - a general theory*. Durham, NC: Duke University Press.

Dählback, N., 1989. A symbol is not a symbol. *Proc. IJCAI'89*, Detroit, MI, 8-14

David, F. N., 1962. *Games, Gods and Gambling* (The origins and history of probability and statistical ideas from the earliest times to the Newtonian era). London: Griffin.

Davis, M., 1958. *Computability and Unsolvability*. New York: McGraw-Hill.

Davis, R., Smith, R., 1983. Negotiation as a metaphor for distributed problem solving. *Artificial Intelligence* 20:63-109

Descartes, R., 1664. *Traité de l'homme*. Paris: M. Clerselier.

Doyle, J. R., 1979. A truth maintenance system. *Artificial Intelligence* 12:231-272

Doyle, J. R., 1983. What is rational psychology? *AI Magazine* 4:50-54

Doyle, J. R., 1988. Probability problems in knowledge acquisition for expert systems, *Knowledge-based Systems* 1 (no. 2):114-120

Dreyfus, H. L., 1972. *What Computers Can't Do: The Limits of Artificial Intelligence*. New York: Harper and Row.

Dreyfus, H. L., 1981. From Micro-Worlds to Knowledge Presentation: AI at an Impasse. In *Mind Design*, ed. J. Haugeland, 161-204. Cambridge, Mass.: MIT Press.

Dreyfus, H. L., Dreyfus, S., 1987. *Mind over Machine: The Power of Human Intuition and Expertise in the Era of the Computer*. New York: Free Press.

Dreyfus, H. L., 1988. The Socratic and Platonic basis of cognitivism. *AI and Society*, 2:99-112

Dubois, D., Prade, H., 1980. Conditioning in possibility and evidence theories—a logical viewpoint. *Proc. Intl. Conf. on Information Processing and Management of Uncertainty in Knowledge-Based Systems*, Urbino/Italy, 401-407

Dubois, D., Prade, H., 1985. Evidence measures based on fuzzy information. *Automatica* 21 (no. 5):547-562

Dubois, D., Prade, H., 1986. Weighted minimum and maximum operations in fuzzy set theory. *Information Sciences* 39:205-211

Dubois, D., Prade, H., 1987. Necessity measures and the resolution principle. *IEEE Trans. on SMC* 17 (no. 3):474-478

Dubois, D., Prade, H., 1988a. An introduction to possibilistic and fuzzy logics. In *Non-Standard Logics for Automated Reasoning*. New York: Academic Press.

Dubois, D., Prade, H., 1988b. Resolution principles, possibility theory and modal logic. *Institute National Polytechnique, Toulouse*, LSI Report, Nr. 297

Dubois, D., Prade, H., 1988c. Conditioning and induction with non-additive probabilities. *Institute National Polytechnique, Toulouse*, LSI Report, Nr. 301

Dubois, D., Prade, H., 1989. Measure-free conditioning, probability and non-monotonic reasoning. *Proc. IJCAI'89*, Detroit, MI, 1110-1114

Duda, R. O., Hart, P. E., Nilsson, N., 1976. Subjective Bayesian methods for rule-based inference systems. *SRI International Technical Note*, Nr. 124

Eccles, J. C., 1976. Brain and free will. In *Consciousness and the Brain*, ed. G. Globus, G. Maxwell and I. Savodnik, 101-123. New York: Plenum Press.

Eccles, J. C., 1980. *The Human Psyche*. Berlin-Heidelberg: Springer.

Edelman, G. M., 1977. Group degenerate selection and phasic reentrant signaling: a theory of higher brain function. In *The Neurosciences: Fourth Study Program*, ed. F. O. Schmitt. Cambridge, Mass.: MIT Press.

Edelman, G. M., Mountcastle, V. B., 1978. *The Mindful Brain, Cortical Organization and the Group-Selective Theory of Higher Brain Function*. Cambridge, Mass.: MIT Press.

Ehrenfels, Ch., 1887. Über Fühlen und Wollen — eine psychologische Studie. *Sitzungsberichte der philosophisch-historischen Klasse der Kaiserlichen Akademie der Wissenschaften*. Wien: Gerold.

Etherington, D., 1988. *Reasoning with incomplete information*. London: Pitman.

Fagin, R., Halpern, J. Y., 1989. Uncertainty, belief and probability. *Proc. IJCAI'89*, Detroit, MI, 1161-1167

Feigenbaum, E. A. and Feldman, J. eds., 1963. *Computers and Thought.* New York: McGraw Hill.

Feynman, R. P., Leighton, R. B., Sands, M., 1963. *The Feynman Lectures on Physics.* Reading, Mass.: Addison Wesley.

Findler, N., Brown, J. S., Lo, R., You, H. Y., 1983. A module to estimate numerical values of hidden variables for expert systems. *Intl. Jrl. Man-Machine Studies* 18 (no. 4):323-335

de Finetti, B., 1959. *Foundations of Probability, Philosophy in the Mid-century.* Florence: La Nuova Italia Editrice.

de Finetti, B., 1987. *Probability, Induction and Statistics.* New York: Wiley.

Fleck, L., 1983. *Erfahrung und Tatsache.* Gesammelte Aufsätze, Red. Schäfer, L., Schnelle, Th., Frankfurt/M.

Flores, F., Winograd, T., 1988. *Understanding Computers and Cognition: A New foundation for Design.* Norwood, NJ: Ablex.

Fodor, J. A., 1976. *The Language of Thought.* Hassocks, Sussex: Harvester Press.

Fodor, J. A., 1983. *The Modularity of Mind: An essay on Faculty Psychology.* Cambridge, Mass.: MIT Press.

Forbus, K. R., de Kleer, J., 1988. Focusing the ATMS. *Proc. AAAI'88,* Saint Paul, Minn., 193-198. San Mateo, CA: Morgan Kaufmann.

Frege, G., 1879. *Begriffsschrift, eine der arithmetischen nachgebildeten Formelsprachen des reinen Denkens.* Halle.

Fu, K. S., 1983. A step towards unification of syntactic and statistical pattern recognition. *IEEE Trans. on PAMI* 5 (no. 2):200-205

Fung, M. R., Chong, Y. C., 1986. Metaprobability and Dempster-Shafer in evidential reasoning. In *Uncertainty in Artificial Intelligence,* ed. L. N. Kanal and J. F. Lemmer, 295-301. Amsterdam: Elsevier.

Galambos, J. A., Abelson, R. P., Black, J. B., 1986. *Knowledge structures*. Hillsdale, NJ: Erlbaum.

Gardner, A. v. d. L., 1987. *An Artificial Intelligence Approach to Legal Reasoning*. Cambridge, Mass.: MIT Press.

Gelfond, M., Lifschitz, V., 1988. Compiling circumscriptive theories into logic programs—preliminary report. *Proc. AAAI'88*, Saint Paul, Minn., vol. 1-2., 455-459. San Mateo, CA: Morgan Kaufmann.

Gelsema, E. S., Kanal, L. N., 1988. *Pattern Recognition and Artificial Intelligence Towards an Integration*. Amsterdam: Elsevier.

Genesareth, M., Nilsson, N., 1986. *Logical Foundations of Artificial Intelligence*. Los Altos, CA: Morgan Kaufmann.

Geroch, R., Hartle, J. B., 1986. *Computability and Physical Theories*. New York: Plenum Press.

Ginsberg, M. L., 1985. Does probability have a place in nonmonotonic reasoning? *Proc. 9th IJCAI'85*, Los Angeles, CA, 1, 107-110

Ginsberg, M. L., 1986. Counterfactuals. *Artificial Intelligence* 30:35-79

Ginsberg, M. L. ed., 1987. *Readings in Nonmonotonic Logic*. Los Altos, CA: Morgan Kaufmann.

Gleick, J., 1987. *Chaos: Making a New Science*. New York: Viking Penguin

Goethe, J. W., 1907. *Maximen und Reflexionen*. Weimar: Max Hecker.

Goodman, I. R., Hung T. Nguyen, 1985. *Uncertainty Models for Knowledge-Based Systems—A Unified Approach to the Measurement of Uncertainty*. Amsterdam: Elsevier.

Goodman, N., 1954. *Fact, Fiction and Forecast*. London: Athlone Press.

Gordon, J., Shortliffe, E. H., 1985. A method for managing evidential reasoning in a hierarchical hypothesis space. *Artificial Intelligence* 26:323-357

Gödel, K., 1931. Über formal unentscheidbare Sätze der Principia Mathematica und verwandter Systeme. *Monatshefte für Mathematik und Physik* 38:173-198

Gregory, R. L., 1967. Will seeing machines have illusions? In *Machine Intelligence*, ed. N. L. Collins and D. Michie, vol. I, 169-180. Edinburgh: Edinburgh University Press.

Gregory, R. L., 1977. *Eye and Brain*. 3rd ed. London: Weidenfeld and Nicolson.

Greiner, R., 1988. Learning by understanding analogies. *Artificial Intelligence* 35:81-125

Greiner, R., Silver, B., Becker, S., Grüninger, M., 1988. A review of machine learning at AAAI'87. *Machine Learning* 3:79-92

Griffith, L., 1982. Three principles of representation for semantic networks. *Journal of the ACM* 7 (no. 3):417-442

Grosof, B. N., 1986. An inequality paradigm for probabilistic knowledge. In *Uncertainty in Artificial Intelligence*, ed. L. N. Kanal and J. F. Lemmer, 259-275. Amsterdam: Elsevier.

Hall, P. R., 1989. Computational approaches to analogical reasoning: a comparative analysis. *Artificial Intelligence* 39 (no. l):39-116

Hallett, G., 1988. *Language And Truth*. New Haven: Yale University Press.

Halpern, J. Y., Moses, Y., 1984. Towards a theory of knowledge and ignorance: preliminary report. *Proc. AAAI Workshop on Non-Monotonic Reasoning*, New Paltz, NY, 125-143

Halpern, J. Y. ed., 1986. *Proc. Conference on Theoretical Aspects of Reasoning about Knowledge*. Los Altos, CA: Morgan Kaufmann.

Halpern, J. Y., 1989. An analysis of first-order logics of probability. *Proc. IJCAI'89*, Detroit, MI, 1375-1381

Halpern, J. Y., Rabin, M., 1987. A logic to reason about likelihood. *Artificial Intelligence* 32:379-406

Hanks, S., McDermott, D., 1986. Default reasoning, nonmonotonic logics and the frame problem. *Proc. AAAI'86*, Philadelphia, 328-333

Hanks, S., McDermott, D., 1987. Nonmonotonic logic and temporal projection. *Artificial Intelligence* 33:279-412

Hanson, N. R., 1958. *Patterns of Discovery*. Cambridge: Cambridge University Press.

Hanson, S. J., Bauer, M. 1989. Conceptual clustering, categorization and polymorphy. *Machine Learning* 3:343-372

Hao Bai-Lin, 1984. *Chaos*. Singapore: World Scientific.

Harel, D., 1987. *Algorithmics. The Spirit of Computing*. Reading, Mass.: Addison-Wesley.

Hartmann, N., 1950. *Philosophie der Natur*. Berlin: Walter d. Gruyter.

Haugeland, J., 1985. *Artificial Intelligence: The Very Idea*. Cambridge, Mass.: MIT Press.

Havel, I. M., 1985. A lesson in human self-understanding. In *Impacts of Artificial Intelligence*, ed. R. Trappl, 87-98. Amsterdam: Elsevier.

Hayes, P. J., 1974. Some problems and non-problems in representation theory. *Proc. AISB Summer Conference*, University of Sussex, 63-79

Hayes, P. J., 1977. In defense of logic. *Proc. IJCAI'77*, 428-433. Cambridge, Mass.: MIT Press.

Hayes, P. J., 1985. Naive Physics 1: Ontology for liquids. In *Formal Theories of the Common Sense World*, ed. J. R. Hobbs and R. C. Moore. Norwood, NJ: Ablex.

Hayes-Roth, B., Hayes-Roth, F., 1979. A cognitive model of planning. *Cognitive Science* 3:275-310

Hájek, P., Valdes, J. J., 1987. Algebraic foundations of uncertainty processing in rule-based expert systems. *Mathematical Institute, Czechoslovak Academy of Sciences*, Report Nr. 28

Hájek, P., 1987. Towards a probabilistic analysis of MYCIN-like expert systems. , *Mathematical Institute, Czechoslovak Academy of Sciences*, Working Paper.

Hebb, D. O., 1949. *The Organization of Behaviour: A Neuropsychological Theory*. New York: Wiley.

Heckerman, D. E., Horvitz, E. J., 1987. On the expressiveness of rule-based systems for reasoning with uncertainty. *Proc. AAAI'87*, Seattle, vol. 1, 121-126. San Mateo, CA: Morgan Kaufmann.

Heckerman, D. E., Horvitz, E. J., 1988. The myth of modularity in rule-based systems for reasoning with uncertainty. In *Uncertainty in Artificial Intelligence*, ed. L. N. Kanal and J. F. Lemmer, vol. 2, 23-24. Amsterdam: Elsevier.

Henkind, S. J., Harrison, M. C., 1988. An analysis of four uncertainty calculi. *IEEE Trans. on SMC* 18 (no. 5):700-713

Hink, R. F., Woods, D. L., 1987. How humans process uncertain knowledge: an introduction for knowledge engineers. *AI Magazine* 8 (no. 3):41-53

Hintikka, J., 1973. *Time and Necessity – Studies in Aristotle's Theory of Modality*. Oxford: Clarendon Press.

Hintikka, J., 1975. Impossible possible worlds vindicated. *Journal of Philosophical Logic* 4:475-484

Hipel, K. W., Fraser, N. M. 1984. *Conflict Analysis: Models and Resolutions*. Amsterdam: Elsevier.

Hillis, W. D., 1987. The connection machine. *Scientific American* 256:86-93

Hofstadter, D. R., 1979. *Gödel, Escher, Bach: an Eternal Golden Braid*. New York: Basic Books.

Hofstadter, D. R., 1985. *Metamagical Themas: Questing for the Essence of Mind and Pattern*. New York: Basic Books.

Holtzman, S. 1989. *Intelligent Decision Systems*, Reading, Mass.: Addison-Wesley.

Honda, N., Sugimoto, F., 1986. Multivariate data representation and analysis by face pattern using facial expression characteristics. *Pattern Recognition* 19:85-93

Hopcroft, J. E., Ullman, J. D., 1979. *Introduction to Automata Theory, Languages And Computation*. Reading, Mass.: Addison-Wesley.

Hopfield, J. J., 1982. Neural networks and physical systems with emergent collective computational abilities. *Proc. National Academy of Sciences, USA*, 79:2554-2558

Hopfield, J. J., Tank, D. W., 1985. Neural computation of decisions in optimization problems. *Biological Cybernetics* 52:141-152

Huang, K., 1984. *I Ching, The Oracle*. Singapore: World Scientific.

Hubel, D. H., Wiesel, T. N., 1944. Sequence regularity and geometry of orientation columns in the monkey striate cortex. *Journal of Computer Neurology* 158:267-293

Hubel, D. H., Wiesel, T. N., 1962. Receptive fields, binocular interaction and functional architecture in the cat's visual cortex. *Journal of Physiology* (London) 160:106-154

Hubel, D. H., Wiesel, T. N., 1979. Brain mechanisms of vision. *Scientific American* 241 (no. 3):150-162

Huffman, D. A., 1971. Impossible Objects as Nonsense Sentences. In *Machine Intelligence*, ed. B. Meltzer and D. Michie, vol. 6, 295-325. Edinburgh: Edinburgh University Press.

Hummel, R., Landy, M., 1988. Evidence as opinion of experts. In *Uncertainty in Artificial Intelligence*, ed. L. N. Kanal and J. F. Lemmer, vol. 2., 43-54. Amsterdam: Elsevier.

Ihara, J., 1987. Extensions of conditional probability and measures of belief and disbelief in a hypothesis based on uncertain evidence. *IEEE Trans. on PAMI* 9 (no. 4):561-568

Jackson, P., 1989. On the semantics of counterfactuals. *Proc. IJCAI'89*, Detroit, MI, 1382-1387

Jaynes, E. T., 1957. Information theory and statistical mechanics. *Physical Reviews* 106:620-630, 108:71-190

Julesz, B., 1981. Textons, the elements of texture perception and their interactions. *Nature* 290:91-97

Kahneman, D., Tversky, A., 1972. Subjective probability: a judgement of representativeness. *Cognitive Psychology* 3:430-454

Kalman, R. E., 1986. The problem of prejudice in scientific modelling. *Proc. European Econometric Meeting*, Budapest, Hungary, 1-12

Kalman, R. E., 1990. *Nine Lectures on Identification, Springer Lecture Notes on Economics and Mathematical Systems*. Berlin-Heidelberg: Springer.

Kanal, L. N., Lemmer, J. F. ed., 1986. *Uncertainty in Artificial Intelligence*. Amsterdam: Elsevier.

Kane, T., 1989. Maximum entropy in Nilsson's probabilistic logic. *Proc. IJCAI'89*, Detroit, MI, 452-457

Kállai, E., 1947. *The Hidden Face of Nature*. Budapest, Hungary: Misztótfalusi (in Hungarian).

Kesevan, H. K., Kapur, J. N., 1989. The generalized maximum entropy principle, *IEEE Trans. on SMC* 19 (no. 5):1042-1052

Kim, J. H., Pearl, J., 1987. CONVINCE: a Conversational Inference Consolidation Engine. *IEEE Trans. on SMC* 17 (no. 2):120-132

Kleene, S. C., 1936. Lambda-definability and recursiveness. *Duke Mathematical Journal* 2

Kleene, S. C., 1952. *Introduction to Metamathematics*. Amsterdam: Elsevier.

Kleene, S. C., 1967. *Mathematical Logic*. Chichester: Wiley.

de Kleer, J., Brown, J. S., 1982. Assumptions and ambiguities in mechanistic mental models. In *Mental Modes*, ed. Gentner, D. and Stevens, A. L. Hillsdale, NJ: Erlbaum.

de Kleer, J., 1986. An assumption-based truth maintenance system. *Artificial Intelligence* 28:197-224

de Kleer, J., 1989. A comparison of ATMS and CSP techniques. *Proc. IJCAI'89*, Detroit, MI, 290-296

Klein, F., 1872. Vergleichende Betrachtungen über neuere geometrische Forschungen (Erlangen), abgedruckt in *Mathematischen Annalen* 48, 1893

Kline, M., 1980. *Mathematics: the Loss of Certainty*. New York: Oxford University Press.

Kneale, W., Kneale, M., 1971. *The Development of Logic*. Oxford: Oxford University Press.

Knuth, D. E., 1973. *The Art of Computer Programming*. Reading, Mass.: Addison-Wesley.

Kohonen, T., 1982. Self-organized formation of topologically correct feature maps. *Biological Cybernetics* 43:59-61

Kolmogoroff, A. N.,* 1933. *Grundbegriffe der Wahrscheinlichkeitsrechnung*. Berlin-Heidelberg: Springer.

---

* The transcription of the Cyrillic changes, we quote the form of the publications.

Kolmogorov, A. N., 1965. Three approaches to the concept of 'the Amount of Information'. *Problems of Information Transmission* 1:1-7

Kolmogorov, A.N., 1968. Logical Basis for information theory and probability theory. *IEEE Trans. on Information Theory* IT-14:662-664

Kolodner, J. L., Riesbeck, Ch.K., 1986. *Experience, Memory and Reasoning.* Hillsdale, NJ: Erlbaum.

Konolige, K., 1985. A computational theory of belief introspection. *Proc. IJCAI'85*, Los Angeles, CA, vol. 1, 502-508

Konolige, K., 1989. On the relation between autoepistemic logic and circumscription. *Proc. IJCAI'89*, Detroit, MI, 1213-1218

Konolige, K., Pollack, M., 1989. Ascribing plans to agents. *Proc. IJCAI'89*, Detroit, MI, 924-930

Kowalski, R., 1974. Predicate logic as programming language. *Proc. IFIP'74*, 569-574. Amsterdam: Elsevier.

Kowalski, R., 1983. Logic programming. *Proc. Information Processing'83*, ed. R. E. A. Mason, 133-145. Amsterdam: Elsevier.

Kripke, S. A., 1971. Semantical considerations on modal logic. In *Reference and Modality*, ed. L. Linsky, 63-72. London: Oxford University Press.

Kripke, S. A., 1972. Naming and necessity. In *Semantics of Natural Languages*, ed. G. Harmon and D. Davidson, 253-355. Dordrecht: Reidel.

Kuhn, T. S., 1962. *The Structure of Scientific Revolutions.* Chicago: University of Chicago Press.

Kyburg, H. E., 1987. Bayesian and non-Bayesian evidential updating. *Artifical Intelligence* 31:271-293

Kyburg, H. E., 1988a. Knowledge. In *Uncertainty in Artificial Intelligence*, ed. L. N. Kanal and J. F. Lemmer, vol. 2. Amsterdam: Elsevier.

Kyburg, H. E., 1988b. Full belief. *University of Rochester, Dept. of Computer Science,* Technical Report, TR-245

Kyburg, H. E., 1988c. Probabilistic inference and probabilistic reasoning. *University of Rochester, Dept. of Computer Science,* Technical Report, TR-248

Kyburg, H. E., 1988d. Probabilistic inference and non-monotonic inference. *University of Rochester, Dept. of Computer Science,* Technical Report, TR-249

Kyburg, H. E., 1988e. Against conditionalization. *University of Rochester, Dept. of Computer Science,* Technical Report, TR-256

Kyburg, H. E., 1988f. Epistemological relevance and statistical knowledge. *University of Rochester, Dept. of Computer Science,* Technical Report, TR-251

Laertius, D., 1862. *de Clarorum Philosophorum Vitis, Dogmatibus et Apophthegmatibus.* Paris: Didot.

Lakatos, I., 1963. Proofs and refutations. *British Journal of Philosophical Science* 14:1-25, 120-139, 221-243, 296-342

Lakatos, I., 1970. Falsification and the methodology of scientific research programmes. In *Criticism and the Growth of Knowledge,* ed. I. Lakatos and A. Musgrave, 91-196. Cambridge: Cambridge University Press.

Lamport, L., Shostak, R., Pease, M., 1982. The Byzantine Generals Problem. *ACM Trans. on Programming Languages and Systems* 4 (no. 3):382-40l

Lee, K., Mahajan, S., 1988. A pattern classification approach to evaluation function learning. *Artificial Intelligence* 36 (no. 1):1-25

Leibniz, G. W., 1768. *Opera Omnia,* ed. L. Dutens

Leibniz, G. W., 1898. *The Monadology and other Philosophical Writings.* Oxford: University Press.

Leibniz, G. W., 1960. *Fragmente zur Logik*. Berlin: Akademie Verlag.

Lemmer, F. J., 1986. Confidence factors, empiricism and the Dempster-Shafer theory of evidence. In *Uncertainty in Artificial Intelligence*, ed. L. N. Kanal and J. F. Lemmer. Amsterdam: Elsevier.

Lemmer, J. F. and Kanal, L. N. eds., 1988. *Uncertainty in Artificial Intelligence*, vol. 2. Amsterdam: Elsevier.

Lenat, B. D., 1977. The ubiquity of discovery. *Artificial Intelligence* 9:275-285

Lenat, B. D., 1982. The nature of heuristics. *Artificial Intelligence* 19:189-249

Lenat, B. D., 1983a. Theory formation by heuristic search. *Artificial Intelligence* 21:31-59

Lenat, B. D., 1983b. Eurisco: A program that learns new heuristics and domain concepts. *Artificial Intelligence* 21:61-98

Levesque, H. J., 1981. The interaction with incomplete knowledge bases: a formal treatment. *Proc. IJCAI'81*, Vancouver, BC, 240-245

Levesque, H. J. and Brachman, R. J. eds., 1985. *Readings in Knowledge Representation*. Los Altos, CA: Morgan Kaufmann.

Levesque, H. J., 1989. A knowledge-level account of abduction. *Proc. IJCAI'89*, Detroit, MI, 1061-1067

Lifschitz, V., 1985. Computing Circumscription. *Proc. IJCAI'85*, Los Angeles, CA, 1: 121-127

Licklider, J. C. R., 1960. Man-machine symbiosis. *IRE Trans. on Human Factors in Electronics* HFE-1

Liu, G.S-H., 1968. Knowledge Structures and Evidential Reasoning in decision analysis. In *Uncertainty in Artificial Intelligence*, ed. L. N. Kanal and J. F. Lemmer, 303-315. Amsterdam: Elsevier.

Lorenz, K., 1981. *The Foundations of Ethology*. New York: Springer.

Lucianus Samosatensis (Rec. Franciscus Fritzschius), 1860-69. Rostock: Ernest Kuhn.

Lucretius, Titus Carus, 1946. *On the Nature of Things* (de Rerum Natura). Transl. Ch.E. Bennett. Roslyn, NY: W. J. Black.

Lukasiewicz, J., 1967. Many-valued systems of propositional logic. In *Polish Logic*, ed. S. McCall. Oxford: Oxford University Press.

Lully, R., 1617. *Opera*. Strasbourg.

McCarthy, J., 1968. Programs with common sense. In *Semantic Information Processing*, ed. M. L. Minsky. Cambridge, Mass.: MIT Press.

McCarthy, J., Hayes, P. J., 1969. Some philosophical problems from the standpoint of artificial intelligence. In *Machine Intelligence*, ed. B. Meltzer and D. Michie, vol. 4, 463-502. Edinburgh: Edinburgh University Press.

McCarthy, J., 1977. Epistemological problems of artificial intelligence. *Proc. IJCAI'77*, 1038-1044. Cambridge, Mass.: MIT Press.

McCarthy, J., 1980. Circumscription: A form of non-monotonic reasoning. *Artificial Intelligence* 13:27-40

McCarthy, J., 1986. Applications of circumscription to formalizing common-sense knowledge. *Artificial Intelligence* 28:89-116

McClelland, J. D., Rumelhart, D. E., 1981. An interactive activation model of context affects in letter perception, Part 1. An account of basic findings. *Psychological Review* 88:375-407

McCullogh, W. S., Pitts, W., 1943. A logical calculus of the ideas immanent in nervous activity. *Bulletin of Mathematical Biophysics* 5:115-137

McDermott, D., 1982. A temporal logic for reasoning about processes and plans. *Cognitive Science* 6:101-155

McDermott, D., Doyle, J. R., 1980. Non-monotonic logic I. *Artificial Intelligence* 13:41-72

Mandelbrot, B., 1977. *The Fractal Geometry of Nature*. New York: Freeman.

Martins, J. P., Shapiro, S. C., 1988. A model for belief revision. *Artificial Intelligence* 35:25-79

Marr, D. C., 1977 Artificial intelligence: a personal view. *Artificial Intelligence* 9:37-48

Marr, D. C., Poggio, T., 1979. A Computational Theory of Human Stereo Vision. *Proc. Royal Society of London* Series B, 204:301-328

Marr, D. C., 1982. *Vision: A Computational Investigation into the Human Representation and Processing of Visual Information*. San Francisco: Freeman.

Marr, D.C., 1985. *Vision*. New York: Wiley.

Maturana, H. R., Varela, F. J., 1988. *Autopoiesis and Cognition*. London: Reidel.

Mendel, M. B., Sheridan, T. B., 1989. Filtering information from human experts. *IEEE Trans. on SMC* 36 (no. 1):6-16

Mérő, L., 1990. *Ways of Thinking. The Limits of Rational Thought and Artificial Intelligence*. Singapore: World Scientific.

Mérő, L., A Fechnerian framework for both Fechner's and Stevens' psychophysical theory, to be published in *Mathematical Psychology*

Michalski, R. S., Carbonell, J. G. and Mitchell, T. M. eds., 1983. *Machine Learning: An Artificial Intelligence Approach*, vol. 1. Palo Alto, CA: Tioga.

Michalski, R. S., 1983b. A theory and methodology of inductive learning. *Artificial Intelligence* 20:111-161

Michalski, R. S., Dietterich, T. G., 1985. Discovering patterns in sequences of event, *Artificial Intelligence* 25:187-232

Michalski, R.S., Carbonell, J. G. and Mitchell, T. M. eds., 1986. *Machine Learning: An Artificial Intelligence Approach*, vol. 2. Los Altos, CA: Morgan Kaufmann.

Michie, D., 1988. Machine learning in the next five years. *Proc. 3rd European Working Session on Learning*, Turing Institute, Glasgow, ed. D. Sleeman, 107-122. London: Pitman.

Minsky, M. L., 1961. Steps toward artificial intelligence. *Proc. Institute of Radio Engineers* 49:8-30

Minsky, M. L., 1975. A framework for representing knowledge. In *The Psychology of Computer Vision*, ed. P. H. Winston, 211-277. New York: McGraw Hill.

Minsky, M. L., Papert, S., 1973. *Artificial Intelligence*. London Lectures, Oregon State System of Higher Education. Eugene, Oregon.

Mitchell, T. M., Carbonell, J. G. and Michalski, R. S. eds., 1986. *A Guide to Current Research*. Boston-Dordrecht: Kluwer Academic Publ.

Montague, R., 1974. *Formal Philosophy* — Selected Papers. New Haven: Yale University Press.

Moore, R. C., 1985. Semantic considerations on nonmonotonic logic. *Artificial Intelligence* 25 (no. 1):75-94

Myhill, J. R., 1951. On the ontological significance of the Löwenheim-Skolem theorem. In *Academic Freedom, Logic and Religion*, ed. M. White. Philadelphia: The University of Pennsylvania Press.

von Neumann, J., Morgenstern, D., 1947. *Theory of Games and Economic Behaviour*. Princeton: Princeton University Press.

von Neumann, J., 1958. *The Computer and the Brain*. New Haven: Yale University Press.

von Neumann, J., 1949. Recent Theories of Turbulence. In *Collected Works*, 1963, ed. A. H. Taub. Oxford: Pergamon Press.

Newell, A., 1982. Intellectual issues in the history of artificial intelligence. Report of *Carnegie-Mellon University, Department of Computer Science, Pittsburgh, PA*, Report, CMU-CS-82-142

Newell, A., Simon, H. A., 1961. GSP – a program that simulates human thought. In *Lernende Automaten*, ed. H. Billing, 109-124. Munich: Oldenbourg.

Newell, A., Simon, H. A., 1972. *Human Problem Solving*. Englewood Cliffs, NJ: Prentice-Hall.

Nilsson, N., 1980. *Principles of Artificial Intelligence*. Palo Alto, CA: Tioga.

Nilsson, N., 1986. Probabilistic logic. *Artificial Intelligence* 28:71-87

Oatley, K., 1989. The importance of being emotional. *New Scientist* 19 August, 33-36

Ockham, W., 1675. *Summa Totius Logicae*. Oxford.

Pao, Y., 1986. Use of qualitative knowledge in learning system behaviour and discovering control strategy. *Proc. SOCOCO'86*, Graz, 4-7

Pearl, J., 1987. Distributed revision of composite beliefs. *Artificial Intelligence* 33: 173-215

Pearl, J., 1986. Fusion, propagation and structuring in belief networks. *Artificial Intelligence* 29:241-288

Pearl, J., 1988. *Probabilistic Reasoning in Intelligent Systems: Networks of Plausible Inference*. San Mateo, CA: Morgan Kaufmann.

Penrose, R., 1989. *The Emperor's New Mind*. Oxford: Oxford University Press.

Perez, A., 1988. To what extent a Markovian approximation of a process is justified knowing only its first-order transition probabilities. *Proc. 4th Prague Symposium on Asymptotic Statistics*. Prague: Charles University.

Perez, A., 1989. Failing of the Dempster's combining rule of interval-given probabilities as applied in expert systems. *Proc. AI'89*, Prague 51-58

Perlis, D., 1988. Languages with self-reference II: knowledge, belief and modality. *Artificial Intelligence* 34:179-212

Péter, R., 1967. *Recursive Functions*. Budapest: Akadémiai Kiadó.

Piaget, J., 1954. *The Construction of Reality in the Child*. New York: Ballantine Books.

Piaget, J., 1952. *The Origins of Intelligence in the Child*. London: Routledge and Kegan Paul.

Piaget, J., 1960. *Psychology of Intelligence*. New York: Littlefield.

Piaget, J., 1976. *The Child and Reality: Principles of Genetic Epistemology*. New York: Penguin.

Plato, 1899. *Opera*. Ed. J. Burnet, Oxford.

Plato, 1573. *Cratylus* — Platonis Opera. Ed. J. Stephanos, Paris.

Poggio, T., Reichardt, W., 1973. A theory of the pattern induced flight orientation in the fly Musca Domestica. *Kybernetik* 12:185-203

Poincaré, H., 1892. *Les Méthodes Nouvelles de la Mechanique Céleste*, vol. 1-3. Paris: Gauthier-Villars.

Polányi, M., 1964. *Personal Knowledge: Towards a Post-Critical Philosophy*. New York: Harper.

Polányi, M., 1965. *The Tacit Dimension*. New York: Doubleday.

Pólya, G., 1945. *How to solve it? A new Aspect of Mathematical Method*. New York: Doubleday.

Popper, K., 1963. *Conjectures and Refutations: The Growth of Scientific Knowledge*. London: Routledge and Kegan Paul.

Prade, H., 1985. A computational approach to approximate and plausible reasoning with applications to expert systems. *IEEE Trans. on PAMI* 7 (no. 3):260-283

Prigogine, I., 1976. Order through fluctuation: self-organization and social systems. In *Evolution and consciousness*, ed. E. Jantsch and D. H. Waddington, 93-133. London: Addison-Wesley.

Provan, G., 1989. An analysis of ATMS-based techniques for computing Dempster-Shafer belief functions. *Proc. IJCAI'89*, Detroit, MI, 1115-1127

Przymusinski, T. C., 1989. An algorithm to compute circumscription. *Artificial Intelligence* 38:49-73

Putnam, H., 1975. *Mind, Language and Reality*. Cambridge: Cambridge University Press.

Putnam, H., 1981. *Reason, Truth and History*. Cambridge: Cambridge University Press.

Pylyshyn, Z. W., 1981. The imagery debate: analogue media versus tacit knowledge. *Psychological Review* 88:16-45

Pylyshyn, Z. W., 1984. *Computation and Cognition: Toward a Foundation for Cognitive Science*. Cambridge, Mass.: MIT Press.

Quillian, M. R., 1968. Semantic Memory. In *Semantic Information Processing*, ed. M. Minsky, 227-270. Cambridge, Mass.: MIT Press.

Quine, W. V. O., 1950. *Methods of Logic*. New York: Henry Holt.

Quine, W. V. O., 1960. *Word and Object*. Cambridge, Mass.: MIT Press.

Quine, W. V. O., 1961. *From a Logical Point of View*. Cambridge, Mass.: Harvard University Press.

Quinlan, J. R., 1979. Discovering rules from large collections of examples: a case study. In *Expert Systems in the Micro-Electronic Age*, ed. D. Michie, 168-201. Edinburgh: Edinburgh University Press.

Quinlan, J. R., 1982. Semiautonomous acquisition of pattern-based knowledge. In *Machine Intelligence*, D. Michie ed., vol. 10, 159-172. Chichester: Ellis Horwood.

Ramsay, F. P., 1931. *The Foundations of Mathematics and Other Logical Essays*. London: Kegan Paul.

Reinfrank, M., Dressler, O., Brewka, G., 1989. On the relation between truth maintenance and autoepistemic logic. *Proc. IJCAI'89*, Detroit, MI, 1206-1212

Reiter, R., 1980. A logic for default reasoning. *Artificial Intelligence* 13:1-2, 81-132

Rendell, L., 1988. Learning Hard Concepts. *Proc. 3rd European Working Session on Learning*, Turing Institute, Glasgow, ed. D. Sleeman, 177-200. London: Pitman.

Rescher, N., 1969. *Many-valued Logic*. New York: McGraw-Hill.

Robinson, J. A., 1965. A machine oriented logic based on the resolution principle. *The Journal of the ACM* 12:23-41

Rosenblatt, F., 1958. The perceptron: a probabilistic model for information storage and organization in the brain. *Psychological Review* 65:386-407

Rosser, J. B., 1984. Highlights of the history of the lambda-calculus. *Annales of the History of Computing* 6:227-349

Rumelhart, D. E., McClelland, J. C., PDP Research Group eds., 1986. *Parallel Distributed Processing*. Cambridge, Mass.: MIT Press.

Ruspini, E. H., 1973. New experimental results in fuzzy clustering. *Information Sciences* 6:273-284

Russell, B., 1945. *History of Western Philosophy*. London: Allen and Unwin.

Ruzsa, I., 1981. *Modal Logic with Descriptions*. Budapest: Akadémiai Kiadó.

Sage, A.P.,1987. Information systems engineering for distributed decisionmaking *IEEE Trans. on SMC* 17 (no. 6):920-936

Salmon, N., 1986. Reflexivity. *Notre Dame Journal of Formal Logic* 27 (no. 3):401-429

Sandewall, E., 1985. A functional approach to non-monotonic logic. *Proc. 9th IJCAI'85*, Los Angeles, CA, 100-106

Savage, L. J., 1954. *The Foundations of Statistics*. New York: Wiley.

Scarrott, G. G., 1988. Physical uncertainty, life and practical affairs. *Journal of Information Technology* 3:58-61

Scarrott, G. G., 1989. The nature of information. *The Computer Journal* 32:262-266

Schank, R. C., 1984. *The Cognitive Computer on Language, Learning and Artificial Intelligence*. Reading, Mass.: Addison-Wesley.

Schank, R. C., 1972. Conceptual dependency: a theory of natural language understanding. *Cognitive Psychology* 3:552-631

Schank, R. C., Abelson, R. P., 1977. *Scripts, Plans, Goals and Understanding*. Hillsdale, NJ: Erlbaum.

Schank, R. C., 1982. Reminding and memory organization: an introduction to MOPS. In *Strategies for Natural Language Processing*, ed. W.G. Lehnert and M. H. Ringle, 455-494. Hillsdale, NJ: Erlbaum.

Schank, R. C., Childers, P., 1984. *The Cognitive Computer: On Language, Learning and Artificial Intelligence*. Reading, Mass.: Addison-Wesley.

Schank, R. C., 1986. *Explanation Patterns: Understanding Mechanically and Creatively*. Hillsdale, NJ: Erlbaum.

Schocken, S., Kleindorfer, P. R., 1989. Artificial intelligence dialects of the Bayesian belief revision language. *IEEE Trans. on SMC* 19 (no. 5):1106-1121

Searle, J. R., 1980. Minds, brains and programs. *Behavioral and Brain Sciences* 3:417-457

Searle, J. R., 1990. Is the brain's mind a computer program? *Scientific American* 1:20-25

Selfridge, O. G., 1959. Pandemonium: a paradigm for learning. *Proc. Symposium on Mechanisation of Thought Processes*, ed. D. V. Blake and A. M. Uttley, 511-529. London: H. M. Stationery Office.

Sextus Empiricus, *Opera*. Ed. H. Mutschmannn and I. Man, Leipzig, 1912-1954

Shafer, G., 1976. *A Mathematical Theory of Evidence*. Princeton: Princeton University Press.

Shafer, G., 1986. Probability judgement in artificial intelligence. In *Uncertainty in Artificial Intelligence*, ed. L. N. Kanal and J. F. Lemmer, 127-135. Amsterdam: Elsevier.

Shafer, G., Logan, R., 1987a. Implementing Dempster's rule for hierarchical evidence. *Artificial Intelligence* 33:271-298

Shafer, G., Lindley, D. V., Spiegelhalter, D. J., 1987b. Uncertainty in expert systems — discussion. *Statistical Science* 2:3-44

Shastri, L., Feldman, J., 1985. Evidential reasoning in semantic networks. *Proc. 9th IJCAI'85*, Los Angeles, CA, 1, 466-474

Shoham, Y., Moses, Y., 1989. Belief as defeasible knowledge. *Proc. IJCAI'89*, Detroit, MI, 1168-1173

Shoham, Y., 1988. *Reasoning about Change*. Cambridge, Mass.: MIT Press.

Sloman, A., 1987. *The Computer Revolution in Philosophy: Philosophy, Science and Models of Mind*. Brighton: Harvester Press.

Sloman, A., 198., What enables a machine to understand? *Proc. IJCAI'85*, Los Angeles, CA, vol. 2, 995-1001

Sloman, A., 1986. Reference without causal links. *Proc. 7th European Conference on Artificial Intelligence*, ed. B. du Boulay and L. J. Steels. Amsterdam: Elsevier.

Smets, P., Mamdani, E., Dubois, D. and Prade, H. eds., 1988. *Non-Standard Logics for Automated Reasoning*. London: Academic Press.

Smolensky, P., 1987. Connectionist AI, symbolic AI and the brain. *AI Review* 1:95-110

Smolensky, P., 1988. On the proper treatment of connectionism. *Behavioral and Brain Sciences* 11:1-74

Sompolinsky, H., 1988. Statistical mechanics of neural networks. *Physics Today* December, 70-79

Sowa, J. F., 1984 *Conceptual Structures: Information Processing in Mind and Machine*. Reading, Mass.: Addison-Wesley.

Spiegelhalter, D. J., 1986. Probabilistic reasoning in predictive expert systems. In *Uncertainty in Artificial Intelligence*, ed. L. N. Kanal and J. F. Lemmer, 47-68. Amsterdam: Elsevier.

Stalnaker, R. A note on non-monotonic modal logic. Unpublished note, June 1980., referred to in [Thayse, 1988]

Stoyan, H., 1985. *GWAI-85: 9th German Workshop on Artificial Intelligence*. Berlin-Heidelberg: Springer.

Szentágothai, J., 1975. The "module-concept" in cerebral cortex architecture. *Brain Research* 95:475-496

Szentágothai, J., 1978. The neuron network of cerebral cortex: a functional interpretation. *Proc. Royal Society of London*, Serie B, *Biological Sciences* 201:219-248

Szentágothai, J. et al. eds., 1981. Advances in physiological sciences. *Proc. 28th International Congress of Physiological Sciences*, Oxford-Budapest: Pergamon-Akadémiai Kiadó.

Szentágothai, J., 1983. The modular architectonic principle of neural centers. *Review of Physiological Pharmacology* 98:11-61

Tarski, A., 1956. *Logic, Semantics, Metamathematics*. Oxford: Clarendon Press.

Thayse, A. ed., 1988. *From Standard Logic to Logic Programming.* Chichester: Wiley.

Turing, A. M., 1936. On computable numbers, with an application to the Entscheidungsproblem. *Proc.London Mathematical Society* Series 2, 42:230-265

Turing, A. M., 1937. Computability and lambda-definability. *Journal of Symbolic Logic*, 2:153-163

Turing, A. M., 1950. Computing machinery and intelligence. *Mind* 59:443-460

Tsotsos, J. K., 1989. The complexity of perceptual search tasks. *Proc. IJCAI'89*, Detroit, MI, 1-17

Tversky, A., Kahneman, D., 1974. Judgement under uncertainty: heuristics and biases. *Science* 125:1124-1131

Tversky, A., 1977. Features of similarity. *Psychological Review* 84:327-352

Tversky, A., Slovic, P., Kahneman, D., 1982. *Judgement under Uncertainty: Heuristics and Biases.* Cambridge: Cambridge University Press, 47-519

Tversky, A., Kahneman, D., 1983. Extensional versus intuitive reasoning: the conjunction fallacy in probability judgements. *Psychological Review* 90:293-315

Valiant, L. G., 1984. A theory of the learnable. *Journal of the ACM* 4:436-445, 1987, *CACM* 27:1134-1142

Valiant, L. G., 1985. Learning disjunctions of conjunctions. *Proc. IJCAI'85*, Los Angeles, CA, 560-565

Valiant, L. G., 1988. Functionality in neural nets. *Proc. AAAI'88*, Saint Paul, Minn., vol. 1-2., 629-634. San Mateo, CA: Morgan Kaufmann.

Walley, P., 1987. Belief function representations of statistical evidence. *The Annals of Statistics* 15 (no. 4):1439-1465

Waterman, D. A. and Hayes-Roth, F. eds., 1978. *Pattern-Directed Inference Systems*. New York: Academic Press.

Weischedel, R., 1986. Knowledge representation and natural language processing. *Proc. IEEE* 74 (no. 7):905-919

Weizenbaum, J., 1976. *Computer Power and Human Reason*. San Francisco: Freeman.

Weyhrauch, W. R., 1980. Prolegomena to a theory of mechanized formal reasoning. *Artificial Intelligence* 13:133-170

Wilkins, D. C., 1988. Knowledge base refinement using apprenticeship learning techniques. *Proc. AAAI'88*, Saint Paul, Minn., vol. 1-2., 646-653. San Mateo, CA: Morgan Kaufmann.

Winograd, T., 1972. *Understanding Natural Language*. New York: Academic Press.

Winograd, T., 1983. *Language as a Cognitive Process: Syntax*. Reading, Mass.: Addison-Wesley.

Winograd, T., Flores, F., 1986. *Understanding Computers and Cognition: A New Foundation for Design*. Norwood, NJ: Ablex.

Winston, P. H., 1970. *Learning structural descriptions from examples*. Doctoral Dissertation. Cambridge, Mass.: MIT Press.

Winston, P. H., 1982. Learning new principles from precedents and exercises. *Artificial Intelligence* 19:321-350

Wise, P. B., Henrion, M., 1986. A framework of comparing inference systems to probability. In *Uncertainty in Artificial Intelligence*, ed. L. N. Kanal and J. F. Lemmer, 69-83. Amsterdam: Elsevier.

Wittgenstein, L., 1922. *Tractatus Logico-Philosophicus*. London: Routledge and Kegan Paul.

Wittgenstein, L., 1953. *Philosophical Investigations*. New York: MacMillan.

Wolff-Terroine, M., 1976. Metalanguages in medicine. *Medical Information* 1 (no. 1):5-14

Yager, R. R., 1986. A modification of the certainty measure to handle subnormal distributions. *Fuzzy Sets and Systems* 20:317-324

Zadeh, L. A., 1965. Fuzzy sets. *Information and Control* 8:338-353

Zadeh, L. A., 1968. Probability measures of fuzzy events. *Journal of Mathematical Analysis and Application* 23:421-427

Zadeh, L. A., 1978a. Fuzzy sets as a basis for a theory of possibility. *Fuzzy Sets and Systems* 1 (no. 1):3-28

Zadeh, L. A., 1978b. PRUF—a meaning representation language for natural languages. In *Man-Machine Studies*, vol. 10., 395-460. New York: Academic Press.

Zadeh, L. A., 1981. Test-score semantics for natural languages and meaning representation via PRUF. In *Empirical Semantics*, ed. B. Rieger, vol. I, 284-349. Bochum: Brockmeyer.

Zadeh, L. A., 1983. A computational approach to fuzzy quantifiers in natural languages. *Computers and Mathematics with Applications* 9:149-184

Zadeh, L. A., 1985. Syllogistic reasoning in fuzzy logic and its application to reasoning with dispositions. *IEEE Trans. on SMC* 15 (no. 6):754-763

Zadeh, L. A., 1986. Is probability theory sufficient for dealing with uncertainty in AI? A negative view. In *Uncertainty in Artificial Intelligence*, ed. L. N. Kanal and J. F. Lemmer, 103-115. Amsterdam: Elsevier.

Zadeh, L. A., 1989. Knowledge representation in fuzzy logic. *IEEE Trans. on Knowledge and Data Engineering* 1 (no. 1):89-100

Zimmer, A. C., 1984. A model for the interpretation of verbal predictions. *International Journal of Man-Machine Studies* 20:121-143

Zlotkin, J., 1989. Negotiation and task sharing among autonomous
agents in cooperative domains. *Proc.IJCAI'89*, Detroit, MI, 912-917

Name index

Subject index

A

Ace of Spades paradox 92, 180
Achilles and the turtle 79
affirmation 48
Age of Reason 2, 20, 32, 33, 129, 131, 161
algorithmic complexity 22
allied generals 84
ambiguities 116
analogy 152
a priori 170
a posteriori 170
Arabic-medieval 137
Aristotelean logic 70, 73, 179
Arthur-Merlin games 25, 26
Assumption-Based Truth Maintenance Systems (ATMS) 180
autoepistemic logic 69, 179
automata theory 96

B

Barbara syllogism 70
Barwise-Perry logic 74
Bayesian method 30, 41, 42, 43, 48, 54, 58, 59, 60, 65, 66, 67, 94, 138, 170, 171
Bible 5, 32, 102, 123, 129, 131, 141
binding 77, 78
bioengineering 39
block world 83
brain 17, 22, 57, 107, 109, 128, 131, 135, 142, 144, 155, 158, 159

Brownian motion 33
Butterfly Effect 34
Byzantine Generals 84

C

cardinality 24
carpenter and the geometer 120
categories 113
causal 89, 96, 97
Certainty Factor 30, 42, 51, 58, 66, 174
chaotic 2, 27, 34
chess 138, 139, 154
Chinese characters 141, 155
circumscription 69, 80, 90, 95, 97, 177, 178
closed world 48, 57, 82, 83, 85, 87, 89, 118, 119, 123, 177, 179
clustering 148
cognitive psychology 46, 50, 107, 127, 132, 133, 136, 140, 149, 161
coin or dice 36
combination 48, 57, 59, 92
communication revolutions 9, 10, 11
complexity 13, 21, 22, 23, 24, 27, 50, 56, 106, 129, 142, 146, 154, 155, 157
concept 113, 123
confidence 38, 45, 56, 61
connectionist theory 158
contradictions 161
control system 145
convergence of models and methods 19, 20, 24, 37, 41, 50, 55
convex geometry 168
cosmogony 39